Leading the Use of Research and Evidence in Schools

IOEPress

Leading the Use of Research and Evidence in Schools

Edited by Chris Brown

Institute of Education Press

First published in 2015 by the Institute of Education Press, UCL Institute of Education, University College London, 20 Bedford Way, London WC1H 0AL

ioepress.co.uk

British Library Cataloguing in Publication Data:
A catalogue record for this publication is available from the British Library

ISBNs
978-1-78277-111-1 (paperback)
978-1-78277-112-8 (PDF eBook)
978-1-78277-113-5 (ePub eBook)
978-1-78277-114-2 (Kindle eBook)

Every effort has been made to trace copyright holders and to obtain their permission for the use of copyright material. The publisher apologizes for any errors or omissions and would be grateful if notified of any corrections that should be incorporated in future reprints or editions of this book.

The opinions expressed in this publication are those of the author and do not necessarily reflect the views of the UCL Institute of Education, University College London.

Typeset by Quadrant Infotech (India) Pvt Ltd
Printed by CPI Group (UK) Ltd, Croydon, CR0 4YY

Cover image ©Thinkstock.com/Fuse

Contents

List of figures

List of tables

For Pete Jonas, who models what it means to love knowledge on a daily basis.

Acknowledgements

This book would not exist without the willingness and efforts of its able contributors, so first huge thanks to each and every one of them for making it possible. Beyond this, I would like to express my gratitude to Professor Louise Stoll for asking me to join her in bidding for and working on our ESRC-sponsored project, which examined the potential of middle leaders to be 'catalysts' for evidence-informed change (see Chapter 6). Similar gratitude goes to Professor Sue Rogers in relation to our work together on the Camden Early Years cluster (see Chapter 7). Thanks also to Paul Phillips and Lorna Ponambalum, who took time to read and comment on early drafts of the book. I also thank Lorna more generally, simply for putting up with me during our work on the Camden Primary to Secondary Transition Lesson Study project.

During the course of bringing together this book I have cultivated a number of excellent relationships with people willing to help mentor and cultivate my efforts. Highlighting two of these, I would like especially to thank Alan Daly and Karen Spence-Thomas for support that goes above and beyond the call of duty.

Finally, thank you to my family for continuing to make life meaningful and for dealing with my grumpiness over a tricky 12 months.

About the contributors

Tom Bennett is the Director of researchED, an organization that seeks to bring together teacher-practitioner and research communities in purposeful and productive dialogue. A full-time teacher in the east end of London, he is also the author of four popular teacher training books, including *Teacher Proof*, a debunking of some of education's mythical and cargo-cult science. A former Teacher Fellow of Corpus Christi College, University of Cambridge, he writes every week for the TES and regularly appears in the media talking about issues that affect teachers.

Chris Brown (editor) is Lecturer in Evidence Informed Policy and Practice in the London Centre for Leadership in Learning (LCLL), UCL Institute of Education (IOE). With a long-standing interest in how evidence can aid the development of policy and practice, Chris has written two books (including *Making Evidence Matter*), several papers, and has presented on the subject at a number of international conferences in Europe and North America. Chris has extensive experience of leading a range of funded projects, many of which seek to help practitioners to identify and scale up best practice. In 2015 he won the Educational Change Special Interest Group Emerging Scholars Award, and has been awarded a significant grant by the Education Endowment Foundation to work with more than a hundred primary schools in England to increase their use of research.

Jing Che, PhD is an Educational Data Strategist at the Rochester City School District and a Data Fellow at the Strategic Data Project, Center for Education Policy Research, Harvard University. Her areas of focus include research and teaching in the fields of English to Speakers of Other Languages, quantitative research, and educational policy analysis. She received her PhD in education from the University of Rochester.

Alan J. Daly, PhD is Professor and Chair of the Department of Education Studies at the University of California, San Diego. He graduated from Clark University with a bachelor of arts in psychology, received a master's of science in counseling from San Diego State University, and a master's of arts and PhD in education with an emphasis on educational leadership and organizations from the University of California, Santa Barbara. Prior to coming to the university, Alan gained over 16 years of public education experience in a variety of positions ranging from classroom teacher to district psychologist to site administrator, providing him with a solid grounding in the world of practice. Alan has presented at the local, state, national, and international level regarding his practical and research work in organizational learning, policy implementation, social networks, and educational reform. His research and teaching primarily focus on social network theory and analysis, leadership, educational policy, and evidence use.

Lorna Earl is a retired Associate Professor from the Ontario Institute for Studies in Education, University of Toronto and is currently President, Lorna Earl and Associates and a part-time Professor at the University of Auckland. Her areas of research include assessment, using data for decision making, evaluation methods, knowledge mobilization, and networking for school improvement.

Kara S. Finnigan, PhD is Associate Professor of Education Policy at the University of Rochester's (UR) Warner School of Education. She has conducted research and evaluations of K-12 policies and programmes at the local, state, and federal level for more than twenty years through her work at UR and prominent research organizations, including the Wisconsin Center for Education Research, SRI International, RPP International, and the George Lucas Educational Foundation. She has written extensively on the topics of low-performing schools and high-stakes accountability, district reform, principal leadership, and school choice. Finnigan's research blends perspectives in education, sociology, and political science; employs qualitative and quantitative methods, including social network analysis; and focuses on urban school districts. She recently served as Associate Editor of the American Educational Research Journal (AERJ). Finnigan received her PhD in education policy from the University of Wisconsin–Madison, her MA in administration and policy analysis from Stanford University, and a BA from Dartmouth College.

Hélène Galdin-O'Shea has been a teacher, primarily of English, for 17 years and has led the teaching of media studies at A Level for the last 8 years. Hélène has the role of Research Advocate at her school, is part of the Continuing Professional Development team, championing lesson study in particular and facilitating the work done by staff enquiry groups. Outside of school, she spends much of her time organizing TeachMeets and conferences, notably Pedagoo London, #TMCollaborate (a joint effort), and the researchED events with Tom Bennett. Hélène is always in awe of the generosity with which teachers share their practice and their willingness to learn from one another, and she is keen to do anything to facilitate that. Hélène is interested in promoting cross-institution pedagogic collaboration as part of professional development, in support of teachers who, tired of top-down and often poorly informed initiatives in schools, have rightly decided to reclaim their professionalism and take control of their own development. She is also keen on promoting and developing ways for educational professionals to share the best evidence available. On Twitter, she is @hgaldinoshea and @parkhighmedia.

Professor Toby Greany joined the London Centre for Leadership and Learning at the UCL Institute of Education (IOE) in July 2013. His interests include system reform and system leadership, school leadership and improvement, and the nature and impact of evidence-based practice. Before joining the IOE, Toby was Acting Executive Director: Leadership Development and Director: Research and Development, at the National College for Teaching and Leadership (formerly NCSL) for seven years. In that role he oversaw the college's leadership development provision for school and early years leaders, its policy work, and its research programme. He has worked at the Design Council, the Campaign for Learning, and the Cabinet Office. From 2005 to 2006 he was Special Adviser to the Education and Skills Select Committee. He has a master's in adult education from the University of Manchester, has authored a number of books on schools and education, and has taught in Brazil, China, and the UK.

Nadine Hylton is a PhD student in education policy and theory at the University of Rochester's Warner School of Education. She is currently a Research Assistant for Dr Finnigan's study of low-performing schools and districts using social network analysis and her study of the Urban–Suburban

Interdistrict Transfer Program, which allows students to move across school district boundaries in the Rochester metropolitan area. Her dissertation research focuses on how geography and sociocultural boundaries impact parental participation in school choice.

Clare Roberts trained as a modern foreign languages teacher on the Teach First programme and has been teaching in her school in London for the last three years. Her interest in teacher research derived from her work leading her school's programme of action research and her completion of a part-time master's degree in leadership (Teach First) at the UCL Institute of Education.

Professor Sue Rogers is Head of Early Years and Primary Education at the UCL Institute of Education (IOE). Her research is concerned mainly with pedagogy and expertise in early years education, and the role of play in educational contexts. She has published widely in the field, including three books, and has led a range of funded projects in early years settings and primary schools. Her recent work has deployed Bernstein's theories to understand how policy discourses shape the experience of teachers and young children.

Lesley Saunders is a Visiting Professor at the UCL Institute of Education (IOE), a Research Fellow at the University of Oxford Department of Education, and an Honorary Fellow of the College of Teachers. After qualifying as a teacher, she worked at the National Foundation for Educational Research from 1987 to 2000, where she set up and headed the School Improvement Research Centre. From 2000 to 2008, she was Senior Policy Adviser for Research at the General Teaching Council for England, where she was instrumental in promoting the idea of teaching as a research-informed profession. She started the Special Interest Group on educational research and policymaking for the British Educational Research Association, and served as a user member on the education sub-panel for the UK Research Assessment Exercise 2008. Now an independent research consultant, Lesley has worked for a variety of clients including the World Bank and Save the Children in Kosovo. Lesley has around two hundred sole-authored and co-authored publications and is also an award-winning poet.

Karen Spence-Thomas is Programme Leader for Continuing Professional Development and Aspiring Leaders at the London Centre for Leadership and Learning (LCLL) at the UCL Institute of Education (IOE). She is also Deputy Director for School Partnerships and specializes in developing tailored professional development with school clusters and partnerships. Before joining the IOE, she was a secondary music teacher, a senior leader in London schools, and a local authority adviser. Karen is particularly interested in supporting schools to engage in and with research, and leads the IOE R&D Schools Network with Toby Greany.

Louise Stoll is a former President of the International Congress for School Effectiveness and School Improvement, part-time Professor at the London Centre for Leadership in Learning at the UCL Institute of Education (IOE), and a freelance researcher and international consultant. Her research and development activity focuses on how schools, districts, and national systems create capacity for learning and improvement, with particular emphasis on leadership, learning communities, and learning networks. She also tries to find ways to help connect research and practice, and particularly enjoys working with school principals and other leaders. She is the author and editor of many publications, including *Professional Learning Communities* with Karen Seashore Louis; *It's About Learning (and It's About Time)* with Dean Fink and Lorna Earl; *Changing Our Schools: Linking School Effectiveness and School Improvement* with Dean Fink; and articles on creating capacity for learning, networking between schools, and creative leadership. Her books have been translated into five languages. She also co-edits a book series, Expanding Educational Horizons. Professor Stoll is a keynote presenter, workshop facilitator, and consultant in many countries, and presented a series of *Hot Research* on Teachers' TV in England. She is a member of the governing body of a special school.

Jonathan Supovitz is an Associate Professor of Education Policy and Leadership at the University of Pennsylvania's Graduate School of Education and Co-Director of the Consortium for Policy Research in Education (CPRE). Dr Supovitz is an accomplished mixed-method researcher and evaluator, and lead and co-investigator of numerous nationally funded and foundation-sponsored research projects. He has published findings from numerous educational studies and evaluations of school and district reform efforts. He has presented his work both nationally and internationally on school leadership development and practice; data use and continuous improvement initiatives; and classroom formative assessment practices and state and district test accountability policies. Much of his current research focuses on how school and district leaders create systems for the improvement of teaching and learning.

Carol Taylor currently works at the UCL Institute of Education (IOE), where she is the Strategic Leader PD in the London Centre for Leadership in Learning. She works with schools, alliances, and local authorities – both locally and nationally – in supporting the professional development of the school workforce. Carol was a co-leader of the National College Teaching Schools Research and Development project involving over sixty schools across England, where she was also acting as the external facilitator for a number of Action Learning Sets. She is actively involved in supporting schools across London to embed practitioner research and enquiry into organization and individual practice.

Introduction
Chris Brown

Research and evidence use is a hot topic. With many global school systems now engaging in serious structural changes, administrators, school leaders, and individual teachers are being asked to demonstrate the 'proof' behind their teaching and learning strategies. As a result, the use of research and evidence is now positioned as something vital to providing validity to practice. There is merit in this argument: we know that teacher effectiveness is the most important factor in determining students' outcomes (Rivkin *et al.*, 2005; Barber and Mourshed, 2007; Heck, 2009), with the effects of high-quality teaching being especially significant for pupils from disadvantaged backgrounds. As the Sutton Trust reports (2011), over a given school year disadvantaged pupils gain 1.5 years' worth of learning if taught by very effective teachers, compared with 0.5 years' worth when taught by poorly performing teachers: that is one whole year's worth of learning.

We also know that high-quality Continuous Professional Development (CPD) can have a significant impact on students' learning (e.g. Timperley *et al.*, 2007). This is because the principal way to improve student outcomes is to improve the quality of teachers (Barber and Mourshed, 2007). At the same time, however, a number of studies have found that the vast majority of teacher CPD is ineffective in terms of transforming practice or in leading to improved student outcomes (e.g. Pedder *et al.*, 2010; Sebba *et al.*, 2012a, 2012b). But teachers' engagement with research and evidence, if undertaken in the right way – for example as part of a process of reflective and collaborative professional learning – can not only help teachers improve their practice but can also help the attainment of their pupils (Louis, 2010, 2012; Sebba *et al.*, 2012a, 2012b; Brown and Rogers, 2014).

For a number of reasons, however, many schools have found it difficult to become 'research-engaged', with teachers often lacking the skills, resources, or motivation to use evidence or to undertake meaningful and robust research activity (e.g. Hargreaves, 1996; Cooper *et al.*, 2009; Goldacre, 2013). Responsibility for this sometimes lies with educational academics, who can fail to make their research accessible to teachers, not only in terms of where it is published and the language typically employed, but also in terms of identifying how their research can make a difference (Brown, 2011). But this is not universally the case, and bodies such as the Education Endowment Foundation (EEF) have aimed to make 'what seems to be effective' accessible (one only has to look at the EEF's toolkit for an example of such efforts[1]).

So part of the difficulty also lies with schools. Teachers, for instance, are often not allocated adequate time to explore and share what research exists regarding a particular issue. Or, as a result of the timetabling process, they can find themselves unable to work collaboratively with others to identify and trial ways to address an issue of teaching and learning (Godfrey, 2014). Also, other activities are often prioritized over research-informed professional development, which as a result, and in the face of any desire by teachers to the contrary, can fall down the pecking order of things that need to be attended to. These difficulties are also reflected at a system level – in terms of the collaborative engagement of teachers across schools – and are compounded by other drivers such as the incentive for schools to regard one another as competitors, and accountability systems that promote short-term wins rather than long-term and sustainable improvements in performance (Wilkins, 2011; Cranston, 2013; Godfrey, 2014). These factors all point in the direction of the need for effective school leadership in this area and the plain and simple fact that evidence-informed, self-improving school systems are unlikely to materialize without the active support of school leaders.

The importance of school leadership

The importance of effective school leadership for improving school outcomes is now undisputed (Leithwood *et al.*, 2004; Leithwood and Louis, 2012; Earley, 2013) and a number of key characteristics have been identified as important in relation to effective leadership. These include:

1. providing vision
2. developing, through consultation, a common purpose
3. facilitating the achievement of organizational goals and fostering high performance expectations
4. linking resource to outcomes
5. working creatively and empowering others
6. having a future orientation
7. responding to diverse needs and situations
8. supporting the school as a lively educational place
9. ensuring that the curriculum and processes related to it are contemporary and relevant
10. providing educational entrepreneurship.

(Day and Sammons, 2013: 5)

In themselves, these qualities can be broadly divided into the 'transformational' and the 'learning-centred' aspects of leadership (Day and Sammons, 2013). The first relates to how school leaders align the commitment of those in a school to organizational goals, vision, and direction, and has been shown to have a positive impact in relation to the introduction of new initiatives or the remodelling or restructuring of school activity (e.g. Leithwood, 1994; Bush and Glover, 2003). The second relates to the efforts of school leaders in improving teaching in their school and their focus on the relationships between teachers, as well as on the behaviour of teachers vis-à-vis their work with students. Importantly, it has also been shown that effective learning-centred leadership has substantial benefits for student outcomes, more so in fact that any other approach to leadership (Robinson *et al.*, 2009; Timperley and Robertson, 2011).

Relating these twin aspects of leadership to evidence use has a number of implications for school leaders seeking to capitalize on the benefits of developing a research-engaged school. Specifically, they highlight that school leaders not only need to promote the vision for, and a culture attuned to, evidence use (including the promotion of the values required for learning communities to operate), they also need to provide the necessary resources and structures for sustained and meaningful evidence use to become a reality.

At the same time, it is not always obvious what is required to do these things successfully, and school leaders have traditionally lacked guidance in this area. Correspondingly, the aim of this book is to provide this much-needed support. Written by the key thinkers, writers, and importantly 'doers' in the field, with content designed to address both the transformative and learning-centred aspects of leading evidence use, the book provides new and innovative ideas and suggestions for how schools can become research engaged. Importantly, however, it is also filled with practical material to support school leaders' efforts in this area.

Content

The book begins with a contextual analysis by Toby Greany: 'How can evidence inform teaching and decision making across 21,000 autonomous schools?: Learning from the journey in England'. From Ontario to Australia, and from the US to Europe, schools and policymakers are increasingly focused on how evidence can be better leveraged. Drivers for this change include both economic imperative and new thinking on how school systems should be structured. As Toby notes, however, while millions of pounds have been spent in England over the past twenty years on initiatives aimed at improving evidence-informed practice, it seems that they have had limited impact. Why is this and what are the implications of the current government's push for more autonomous schools and a self-improving system? Toby explores these issues in detail before outlining six emerging claims for mobilizing evidence that reflect findings from a number of recent evidence-use projects, and highlights their implications for policy and practice.

Following Toby's chapter is Tom Bennett's analysis of 'Evidence and quality', an exploration of what is meant by 'good' evidence in the professional context. Designed to provide insight into the types of evidence that should form the basis of research-informed enquiry, Tom's chapter examines the benefits and limitations of evidence produced by both quantitative and qualitative methods. Important too in this regard are notions of quality in relation to prominent methodologies such as randomized controlled trials and action research. Tom also sets out a number of quality pitfalls, including: advocacy disguised as objectivity, research produced to serve political interests, and research published through non-standard routes.

Having explored what good evidence is, and crucially what it is not, the focus of the book turns to how evidence might be used. First, in '"Evidence" and teaching: A question of trust?', Lesley Saunders uses the perspectives of the art, craft, and science of pedagogy as a lens for understanding and articulating the depth and complexity of what teachers know, believe, and do. Lesley rightly remains sceptical of how the concept of evidence use materializes in practice and reminds readers of the need to avoid getting too caught up in the optimism of the evidence-use movement. Recalling that England benefited from a decade or more of 'evidence-based education' under a previous government, she suggests that one of the key lessons from this period is the need for both practitioners and policymakers to have a broader conceptualization of the role of evidence and scholarship in teaching, one that should be integral to the initial and continuing professional development of teachers.

Building on Lesley's chapter, it is clear that processes of learning in relation to evidence are vital in order to create contextually meaningful solutions to issues of practice. Louise Stoll unpacks this issue in her chapter: 'Using evidence, learning, and the role of professional learning communities'. Specifically, she asks 'how can professional learning communities help lead to effective and meaningful learning?'; 'what do we know about how best they should be run?'; and 'what examples do we have for their success?' A specific example of a learning community is then provided in 'Middle leaders as catalysts for evidence-informed change'. Here Louise Stoll and

I examine how we worked with a learning community of school middle leaders (teacher leaders) to develop their understanding of effective middle-leader practice and how they might measure the impact of their approaches to improving the teaching practices of others. Based on the results of the project we argue that middle leaders are often the most effective drivers of evidence-informed change and should be utilized in this way.

Sue Rogers and I provide a second example of professional learning communities in action in 'Knowledge creation as an approach to delivering evidence-informed practice among early years practitioners in Camden (London)'. We argue that, to be done effectively, engaging with evidence requires practitioners to *combine* their understanding of their school context and existing practice with any new understanding this evidence (such as that produced by researchers) provides. Accordingly, we detail how *knowledge-creation* activity enabled us to develop evidence-informed practice among a learning community of 36 early years practitioners in the London Borough of Camden. We also provide ways of measuring evidence use: specifically, we show how we ascertained whether early years practitioners, having been engaged in knowledge-creation activity across a school year, developed *expertise* as evidence users.

As well as engaging with evidence, practitioners also require support in leading their own enquiries. Correspondingly, in 'Leading "disciplined enquiries" in schools', Hélène Galdin-O'Shea sets out a number of case studies of the ways in which teachers lead different kinds of enquiry, both within and between schools. Identifying a range of models and acknowledging the fact that 'practitioner research' is a very broad phrase that is used to refer to many things, from practitioners engaging in research activity to group enquiries where teachers engage with evidence such as school data, Hélène also examines issues that need to be overcome including time and financial constraints, along with suggestions for doing so. The next two chapters build on Hélène's initial analysis.

In the first, 'Impractical research: Overcoming the obstacles to becoming an evidence-informed school', Clare Roberts tells the story of a programme of action research conducted over the course of a year in a UK secondary school. Building on Clare's evaluation of the programme, the chapter highlights where school leaders and teachers ran into difficulties and makes recommendations as to how these could have been avoided. In particular, two issues are highlighted as vital to the successful facilitation of collaborative action research. First is the headteachers' communication of their vision for action research, and ongoing support for the programme, along with structures relating to incentives and accountability. The second issue relates to the resources made available to teachers engaging in action research, both in terms of the time available to them and in terms of their access to published research and expertise.

Next, in 'Teacher data use for improving teaching and learning', Jonathan Supovitz examines how teachers can use school data most effectively. Jonathan argues that classroom data provide teachers with a set of potentially powerful resources to serve the needs of all students. At the same time, these data are unlikely to be meaningfully employed without specific guidance on their use. To address this issue, the chapter describes an intervention from the USA designed to provide teachers with both feedback on their teaching practice *and* facilitated conversations about the connections between their teaching and their students' learning. Crucially, he illustrates how both instructional and student achievement data might be combined into a formative feedback system for teachers that also helps them to target students in developmentally appropriate ways.

What should be clear from reading each of these chapters is that evidence use is only meaningful if it makes a difference – if it leads to change and impact. Carol Taylor and Karen Spence-Thomas address this in their chapter, 'Understanding impact and the cycle of enquiry', where they set out a tried and tested approach to collaborative practitioner enquiry that supports schools in evidencing the difference that engaging in enquiry makes for both teacher and pupil outcomes. Describing how the approach has been applied by Teaching School Alliances (TSAs) involved in the National College Research Themes project between 2012 and 2014, Carol and Karen draw out practical examples and case studies to illustrate how schools have been able to articulate, understand, and evidence change in staff practice and pupil learning with clarity and confidence.

The final three chapters serve to: (1) showcase innovative, cutting edge approaches to understanding how evidence and knowledge flow within and between schools; and (2) draw together the themes explored and the lessons learned. The first of these can be found in Kara Finnigan, Alan Daly, Nadine D. Hylton, and Jing Che's chapter, 'Leveraging social networks for educational improvement', which provides further context and systems-level thinking from a US perspective. Crucially, the chapter provides an introduction to the concept of *social network analysis* and how this new methodological approach can be used to identify how evidence moves around schools/school districts. As well as highlighting the need to better understand how evidence is defined and used by practitioners, their chapter serves to expand our thinking, focusing on the need to consider the network 'structures' that operate between school practitioners and how these can be improved and better harnessed in order to further promote the flow and use of evidence.

Next is Lorna M. Earl's 'Reflections on the challenges of leading research and evidence use in schools'. Lorna, a respected Canadian academic with an extensive background in school data and evidence use, was asked to write a summarizing piece based on her reading of the book's first 11 chapters. Specifically, her task was to identify key themes and to 'gaze into the crystal ball of the future of using evidence in schools'. As a result, Lorna's chapter not only draws on preceding chapters to highlight some of the real complexities of using evidence for decision making by schools, it also sets out effectively some of the issues that schools must attend to if they are to be thoughtful and wise consumers and users of evidence. Finally, in 'Conclusion', the book establishes a substantive and evidence-rich 'checklist' of considerations for school leaders to help guide their efforts in developing their schools as 'evidence-informed'.

Two final points in relation to the book. First, chapters can either be read consecutively or as stand-alone units, meaning that you can engage with the book's content in the way that suits you best. To ensure chapters are as helpful as possible, however, each follows a similar format, with three specific features:

1. All chapters begin with an 'overview' to provide a brief picture of what to expect and so, depending on your needs and the stage that you are at with developing research engagement within your school, an idea of whether you should read the chapter now or return to it later when it might add more insight.
2. Each chapter ends with 'take-out messages', the key points you need to know and carry with you as you move forward.
3. Where pertinent, 'resource boxes' are also provided: these signpost case studies, exemplars, key websites, and other sources of information that will provide assistance as you begin to engage in and with research.

Second, as you can see from the descriptions above, chapters address both engagement 'with' evidence (i.e. teachers using already available evidence to improve their practice) and engagement 'in' evidence-related activity (teachers actively producing evidence, for example through a process of action research). A working definition of 'evidence' can therefore be considered as:

1. 'formal' research produced by researchers
2. the result of practitioner enquiry

3. all quantitative and qualitative data collected on a school's functioning, for example student achievement data and student voice data (e.g. survey data on student well-being).

Point 3 also involves input data (e.g. student characteristics data, such as data on socioeconomic status and truancy), process data (e.g. classroom practices), and context data (e.g. data on school culture and the curriculum) (Stoll *et al.*, forthcoming).

Endnote
[1] See: http://educationendowmentfoundation.org.uk/toolkit/.

References

Barber, M., and Mourshed, M. (2007) *How the World's Best-Performing School Systems Come out on Top*. Online.http://mckinseyonsociety.com/downloads/reports/Education/Worlds_School_Systems_Final.pdf (accessed 11 November 2014).

Brown, C. (2011) 'What Factors Affect the Adoption of Research within Educational Policy Making? How might a better understanding of these factors improve research adoption and aid the development of policy?' Unpublished DPhil diss., University of Sussex.

Brown, C., and Rogers, S. (2014) 'Knowledge creation as an approach to facilitating evidence-informed practice: Examining ways to measure the success of using this method with early years practitioners in Camden (London)'. *Journal of Educational Change*, 16 (1), 79–99. Early online publication. http://link.springer.com/article/10.1007/s10833-014-9238-9 (accessed 19 January 2015; requires subscription).

Bush, T., and Glover, D. (2003) *School Leadership: Concepts and evidence*. Nottingham: National College for School Leadership.

Cooper, A., Levin, B., and Campbell, C. (2009) 'The growing (but still limited) importance of evidence in education policy and practice'. *Journal of Educational Change*, 10 (2–3), 159–71.

Cranston, N. (2013) 'School leaders leading: Professional responsibility not accountability as the key focus'. *Educational Management Administration & Leadership*, 41 (2), 129–42.

Day, C., and Sammons, P. (2013) *Successful Leadership: A review of the international literature*. Reading: CfBT Education Trust.

Earley, P. (2013) *Exploring the School Leadership Landscape: Changing demands, changing realities*. London: Bloomsbury.

Godfrey, D. (2014) 'Leadership of schools as research-led organisations in the English educational environment: Cultivating a research-engaged school culture'. *Educational Management Administration & Leadership*. Early online publication. http://ema.sagepub.com/content/early/2014/02/20/1741143213508294.full (accessed 19 January 2015; requires subscription).

Goldacre, B. (2013) *Building Evidence into Education*. London: Department for Education. Online. http://media.education.gov.uk/assets/files/pdf/b/ben%20goldacre%20paper.pdf (accessed 13 October 2014).

Hargreaves, D. (1996) *The Teacher Training Agency Annual Lecture 1996: Teaching as a Research-Based Profession: Possibilities and prospects*. Online. http://eppi.ioe.ac.uk/cms/Portals/0/PDF%20reviews%20and%20summaries/TTA%20Hargreaves%20lecture.pdf (accessed 14 January 2013).

Heck, R. (2009) 'Teacher effectiveness and student achievement: Investigating a multilevel cross-classified model'. *Journal of Educational Administration*, 47 (2), 227–49.

Leithwood, K. (1994) 'Leadership for school restructuring'. *Educational Administration Quarterly*, 30 (4), 498–518.

Leithwood, K., and Louis, K.S. (2012) *Linking Leadership to Student Learning*. San Francisco, CA: Jossey-Bass.

Leithwood, K., Louis, K.S., Anderson, S., and Wahlstrom, K. (2004) *How Leadership Influences Student Learning*. New York, NY: Wallace Foundation.

Louis, K.S. (2010) 'Better schools through better knowledge? New understanding, new uncertainty'. In Hargreaves, A., Hopkins, D., Fullan, M., and Leiberman, A. (eds) *Second International Handbook of Educational Change*. New York, NY: Springer, 3–28.

— (2012) 'Learning communities in learning schools: Developing the social capacity for change'. In Day, C. (ed.) *International Handbook of Teacher and School Development*. Abingdon: Routledge, 477–92.

Pedder, D., Opfer, V.D., McCormick, R., and Storey, A. (2010) '"Schools and Continuing Professional Development in England – State of the Nation" research study: Policy context, aims and design'. *The Curriculum Journal*, 21 (4), 365–94.

Rivkin, S., Hanushek, E., and Kain, J. (2005) 'Teachers, schools and academic achievement'. *Econometrica*, 73 (2), 417–58.

Robinson, V., Hohepa, M., and Lloyd, C. (2009) *School Leadership and Student Outcomes: Identifying what works and why: Best Evidence Synthesis Iteration (BES)*. Wellington: Ministry of Education.

Sebba, J., Kent, P., and Tregenza, J. (2012a) *Joint Practice Development (JPD): What does the evidence suggest are effective approaches?* Nottingham: National College for School Leadership and University of Sussex.

— (2012b) *Powerful Professional Learning: A school leader's guide to joint practice development*. Online. www.gov.uk/government/uploads/system/uploads/attachment_data/file/329717/powerful-professional-learning-a-school-leaders-guide-to-joint-practice-development.pdf (accessed 26 January 2015).

Stoll, L., Earl, L., Anderson, S., and Schildkamp, K. (forthcoming) 'Changing teachers and teaching: The relationship between educational effectiveness research and practice'. In Chapman, C., Muijs, D., Reynolds, D., Sammons, P., and Teddlie, D. (eds) *Routledge International Handbook of Educational Effectiveness*. London: Routledge.

The Sutton Trust (2011) *Improving the Impact of Teachers on Pupil Achievement in the UK: Interim findings*. Online. www.suttontrust.com/researcharchive/improving-impact-teachers-pupil-achievement-uk-interim-findings/ (accessed 8 November 2014).

Timperley, H., and Robertson, J. (2011) 'Establishing platforms for leadership and learning'. In Robertson, J., and Timperley, H. (eds) *Leadership and Learning*. London: Sage, 3–12.

Timperley, H., Wilson, A., Barrar, H., and Fung, I. (2007) *Teacher Professional Learning and Development: Best Evidence Synthesis Iteration (BES)*. Wellington : Ministry of Education.

Wilkins, R. (2011) *Research Engagement for School Development*. London: Institute of Education Press.

How can evidence inform teaching and decision making across 21,000 autonomous schools?: Learning from the journey in England

Toby Greany

Chapter overview

The evidence that research can impact positively on teacher practice and school improvement is strong. The challenge is how to make it happen. School systems around the world are grappling with this challenge, but there are relatively few evaluations of specific strategies for mobilizing evidence to improve practice.

Millions of pounds have been spent in England over the past twenty years on initiatives aimed at improving evidence-informed practice, yet it seems that they have had limited impact. Why is this? And what are the implications of the current government's push for more autonomous schools and a self-improving system? This chapter will explore these issues, and then conclude by outlining six emerging claims for mobilizing evidence that reflect findings from recent projects in this area, and highlight some of their implications for policy and practice.

The case for developing evidence-informed practice

There are many arguments for why we need an evidence-informed culture in education, but perhaps the strongest comes from cases where research is failing to impact on practice, even though the implications are clear-cut. For example, Levin *et al.* surveyed district leaders and secondary school principals in Canada and found that many are not aware of and/or do not adopt well-evidenced findings (Levin *et al.*, 2011). As a result Levin concludes:

> The injunction to doctors is 'First do no harm'. Yet, because
> schools, groups of schools and indeed whole national systems
> have such weak systems for analysing evidence, it seems likely
> that quite a bit of harm is inadvertently being done.
>
> (Levin, 2013: 20)

More prosaic, but equally important, is the growing correlational evidence that where research and evidence are used effectively as part of high-quality initial teacher education and continuing professional development, with a focus on addressing improvement priorities, it makes a positive difference in terms of teacher, school, and system performance (Mincu, 2014; Cordingley, 2013).

The experience of 'research-engaged' schools that take a strategic and concerted approach in this area is generally positive. Studies suggest that research engagement can shift a school from an instrumental 'top tips' model of improvement to a learning culture in which staff work together to understand what works, when, and why (Godfrey, 2014; Sharp *et al.*, 2006; Handscomb and MacBeath, 2003). That said, there is at least one recent example of an academy where the entire leadership team undertook postgraduate study supported by its university sponsor, yet student outcomes and Ofsted[1] performance both declined. Of course, the two things might not be connected, but it is a reminder that research engagement is not a straightforward panacea in a highly accountable school system.

Despite the arguments in favour of evidence-informed practice, there is a widespread view that education remains backward in this respect, for example when compared with the medical profession (Hargreaves, 1996). The most recent articulation of this view came from Dr Ben Goldacre in his report commissioned by the Department for Education (Goldacre, 2013). Goldacre argued that we need an 'information architecture', including: networks of practitioners to identify relevant research questions; local trials units supporting frequent low-cost randomized controlled trials (RCTs); and 'journal clubs' in schools where practitioners could critique findings from research and develop their understanding of research methods.

Goldacre's core argument that we need more randomized controlled trials in educational research is timely and helpful, but it should not be taken too simplistically. There are genuine arguments about how evidence from different sources and methodologies should be valued and prioritized and the extent to which 'best practice' recommendations can be derived from such reviews (Nutley *et al.*, 2013). Thus, Goldacre's proposed 'information architecture' can be seen as a necessary but not sufficient step if we are to see genuine changes in practice across 21,000 schools (Hemsley-Brown, 2005; Levin *et al.*, 2011).

What can we learn from previous attempts to develop evidence-informed practice in education?

So what can we learn from previous attempts to develop evidence-informed approaches in education? The truth is that many millions of pounds have been spent over the past twenty years on initiatives aimed at addressing the evidence issues facing policy and practice in education, mainly under the 1997 to 2010 New Labour government. One high-profile example is the Teaching and Learning Research Programme (TLRP) which received over £40 million from the Economic and Social Research Council (ESRC) to build the supply of high-quality evidence. There are many more examples and a more comprehensive list is set out in *resource box 1.1*.

RESOURCE BOX 1.1:

Initiatives aimed at addressing the evidence issues facing policy and practice in education include:

- the Teaching and Learning Research Programme (TLRP), which received over £40 million from the Economic and Social Research Council (ESRC) to build the supply of high-quality evidence
- the National Education Research Forum (NERF), which had a remit to develop a strategic approach to evidence-informed practice
- resource banks, such as the Teacher Training Resource Bank (TTRB)
- networks, such as the National Teacher Research Panel (NTRP)
- various schemes that enabled teachers, leaders, schools, and networks to undertake research, such as the Best Practice Research Scholarships scheme and the National College's Research Associates scheme
- funding to support postgraduate study by teachers, in particular the Teacher Training Agency's Postgraduate Professional Development scheme.

In addition to these initiatives, which were overtly aimed at enhancing the supply of high-quality evidence and increasing capacity on the demand-side, the Labour government also spent many millions of pounds more on commissioning and disseminating research, both directly and via large-scale professional development programmes and toolkits. Freedman *et al.* (2008) estimate that Labour invested £342 million in Continuing Professional Development (CPD) programmes for schools in 2007–8 through the National Strategies, Training and Development Agency and local authorities.

What is the evidence of impact from this investment? Of course, it is impossible to assess this in its totality. There is an argument that schools became more data-rich and more evidence-informed over that twenty-year period, but it is hard to attribute this to any specific initiative rather than to, say, the requirements of the accountability system for annual school self-evaluations.

Turning to the evaluations that were undertaken on some of the specific programmes, Nelson and O'Beirne (2014: 14) cite the evaluation of TLRP, which shows relatively limited impact beyond the participating schools, given the scale of investment. In his review of the New Labour initiatives, David Gough (2013) argues that their relative failure to achieve impact was due to a number of factors: they were not given time to bed in; they lacked central coordination; and there was too much emphasis on enhancing the 'push' of research and not enough on increasing demand for research in schools.

Mobilizing knowledge in practice is a messy social process

The limited impact of New Labour's models, which in essence were largely top-down in nature, chimes with some of the wider findings on knowledge mobilization. These show that evidence does not translate into simple, linear changes in practice. Instead, evidence must inform what is ultimately a messy process of social change, whether at the level of the individual practitioner, the school, or the system. Reflecting this fact, many observers have argued that the term 'evidence-based practice' is misleading, preferring terms such as 'evidence-informed practice' and 'knowledge animation' (e.g. Stoll, 2008).

The findings from these studies on knowledge mobilization can be summarized as follows (Brown and Rogers, 2014; Nelson and O'Beirne, 2014; Cordingley, 2013; Nutley *et al.*, 2007; Rycroft-Malone, 2008; Handscomb and MacBeath, 2003; Sharp *et al.*, 2006; Thomas and Pring, 2004; McLaughlin *et al.*, 2004):

- There are widespread concerns about the quality, relevance, and accessibility of much educational research.

- There is a role for clear and accessible research summaries, with a focus on implications and next steps.
- Intermediary bodies and external facilitators are important as they can help busy practitioners to access and engage with evidence.
- Nevertheless, teachers are most likely to trust their peers over other sources, so it is important to consider how informal social networks and peer learning can support knowledge mobilization efforts.
- Even where schools and teachers do access and engage with evidence, they are unlikely to 'apply' the findings in a simplistic or mechanistic way. Evidence must be contextualized and combined with practice-based knowledge (i.e. transformed) as part of a wider collaborative professional learning process.
- Leadership commitment and organizational climate, coupled with practical resources and support (including in terms of time and training), are key factors that influence whether or not teachers will engage with evidence, but many school cultures and systems are not conducive to evidence-informed improvement.
- School- and practitioner-led research and enquiry are dismissed by many (including Goldacre) due to concerns about the small scale and lack of rigour in such approaches. However, the most recent review by the National Foundation for Educational Research (NfER) (Nelson and O'Beirne, 2014) argues that practitioner research can play a range of useful roles, from personal development, to school self-review and improvement, to generating knowledge for the wider system.

What is less clear from this list is that teachers and leaders also face wider barriers to adopting evidence-informed approaches. For example, a survey by the National Teacher Research Panel found that even teachers who value research say that they face a number of challenges in accessing and using evidence, including lack of time, a lack of accessible/practical research summaries, and a lack of support from leaders (National Teacher Research Panel Survey, 2011). The time and workload challenges appear to be particularly acute in England, with evidence that teachers work longer hours and are less likely to engage in sustained professional development than their international peers (Micklewright *et al.*, 2014).

The 'self-improving school-led system' in England: What are the challenges for knowledge mobilization?

New Labour's approach to school improvement and system reform was predominantly top-down, albeit with a significant role for local authorities in both challenging and supporting schools. One indicator of this is that Labour's time in office saw a proliferation in the number of national agencies (quangos) and 'field forces' (teams of consultants charged with roll-out and the implementation of national policy). However, from around 2005 onwards, Labour began to recognize the limitations of top-down reform and sponsored the development of more bottom-up approaches. One example is the National Leaders of Education scheme, which designated successful leaders and schools and then brokered them to support struggling schools (Matthews and Hill, 2008, 2010).

The Coalition government elected in 2010 chose to build on some of Labour's foundations, for example by expanding school-to-school support as the key mechanism for school improvement (Sandals and Bryant, 2014; Earley *et al.*, 2012). However, it would be a mistake to imply that the Coalition's approach is simply an extension of Labour's journey: the differences in philosophy and approach are stark. Specifically, the main theme of the Coalition's approach has been to develop a 'self-improving school-led school system' in which schools are autonomous and accountable, with increased diversity and choice for parents through free schools, and with a radical reduction in central and local oversight. Based on an analysis of the white paper and related documents, I have suggested that the Coalition has four core criteria for the self-improving system (Greany, 2014):

- teachers and schools are responsible for their own improvement
- teachers and schools learn from each other and from research so that effective practice spreads
- the best schools and leaders extend their reach across other schools so that all schools improve
- government support and intervention is minimized.

These criteria signal the importance of partnerships between schools as a key feature of the self-improving system. This is intended to mitigate the risk of stand-alone schools failing, and to address systemic challenges that cannot be addressed by single schools competing against each other. A range of partnership and system leadership models have developed since 2010, but two models have formed the centrepiece of Coalition policy:

- Academy chains: groups of schools that are overseen by a single Multi-Academy Trust (MAT) or, occasionally, an Umbrella Trust. By 2014, more than half of all academies were in a chain, and more than 60 per cent of primary academies (Gu *et al.*, 2014).
- Teaching schools: these are outstanding schools that are designated to coordinate initial and continuing professional development,

school-to-school support, and research and development across an alliance of partner schools (Matthews and Berwick, 2013). By June 2014, 587 teaching schools had been designated.

Thus it can be seen that the architecture of the 'self-improving system' is very different to Labour's model, with significant implications for knowledge mobilization and evidence-informed practice.

Under Labour, the vast majority of schools remained under the influence of their local authority, which had a role in collating and sharing expertise and evidence across schools. The plethora of agencies, toolkits, and training programmes helped ensure that evidence was codified and disseminated nationally. Universities played a key role, leading the bulk of Initial Teacher Training, with significant numbers of teachers undertaking subsidized master's degrees.

By contrast, under the Coalition schools are very clearly in the driving seat:

- the quangos have been closed or stripped back
- local authorities have lost the bulk of their resources and capacity as over 4,000 schools have become academies
- schools are increasingly driving the content and design of Initial Teacher Education through the expansion of School Direct[2]
- teaching schools[3] play a lead role in defining and disseminating effective practice through their research and development function and CPD provision.

This model presents significant opportunities for schools as well as challenges. In terms of the challenges, perhaps the most significant is the emerging evidence that while many schools are seizing the opportunities afforded by the new framework, many others are not. For example, around four in five schools have not yet adopted academy status, while only around half of all schools are expected to be part of a Teaching School Alliance by 2015. Thus there is a risk of a two-tier system emerging, with some schools thriving but others floundering because they do not have access to the knowledge and expertise that they need to improve.

Another challenge is the limited capacity available within schools to take on these new roles. This seems to be particularly true in relation to research and development. The interim evaluation of teaching schools (Gu *et al.*, 2014) reflects considerable progress overall but also flags up the unreasonable and unsustainable workload required to establish the alliances. It states that some alliances see the R&D role as underpinning everything they do and have developed rich relationships with their university partners, but that others have not prioritized R&D, find it daunting, and/or feel that it is underfunded.

One final overarching issue for knowledge mobilization in a self-improving system is the role of school accountability and its impact on competitive behaviours between schools. As other forms of support for schools have been removed and the accountability bar has been consistently raised, there is an argument that England's regime is flattening the very freedom and autonomy that the Coalition seeks to encourage, meaning that schools look to second guess what they think the inspectorate wants to see (rather than looking at the evidence base) and hide their effective practice from their competitor schools (Waldegrave and Simons, 2014).

Conclusion

Jo Rycroft-Malone captures the issues involved in mobilizing evidence perfectly:

> In a contact sport such as ice hockey or rugby, the interaction between a number of different elements determines the nature of the game, the spirit in which it is played, and the ultimate outcome – win or lose. The same could be said of getting evidence into practice: it is the interaction of various ingredients that determines the success of the outcome.
>
> (Rycroft-Malone, 2008: 1)

There are no easy answers when working within a messy social process. Achieving change will take time, commitment, and leadership at many levels: within schools, across schools, and nationally. In some respects the shift to an autonomous self-improving system makes this process harder, but by removing mechanisms for synthesizing and sharing evidence between schools, it also seeks to learn from the pitfalls of a top-down approach by giving greater power to the users of evidence, the schools and teachers who can use it to best effect.

Take-out messages

This section sets out the chapter's take-out messages as a series of emerging claims about knowledge mobilization. It gives examples of schools and initiatives that reflect each of the claims and identifies potential implications for policy and practice. The claims remain tentative: they were developed by the author together with his colleagues at the London Centre for Leadership in Learning (LCLL), Dr Chris Brown and Professor Louise Stoll, and are drawn from a number of studies that the team members have either recently completed or in which they are currently engaged (see chapter appendix):

- **TAKE-OUT** ①: Developing evidence-informed practice within and across schools requires strategic leadership that can shape and implement a shared vision, with clarity on what success looks like, while welcoming complexity and unanticipated outcomes (see *resource box 1.2*).

RESOURCE BOX 1.2:
The Mead Teaching School Alliance in Wiltshire uses a knowledge mobilization framework (Spiral) and has trained Specialist Leaders of Education from across the alliance to support R&D in Innovation Hubs. Further details can be found on the alliance's website (www.themead.wilts.sch.uk/).

Swiss Cottage Teaching School gives teachers one hour a week for R&D, runs a research journal club, and has appointed a Director of R&D. For further details see www.swisscottagedrc.org/.

- **TAKE-OUT** ②: Strategic leadership requires distributed approaches to harnessing knowledge and promoting change. For example, tapping in to social networks (informal leadership) within schools, or finding more formal ways to bring experts and practitioners (or practitioners and others) together (see *resource box 1.3*).

RESOURCE BOX 1.3:
The IOE's Research Learning Communities project, led by Dr Chris Brown, is using a social network analysis questionnaire to identify who the key 'evidence champions' are within participating primary schools. The project will test the effectiveness of these champions in mobilizing evidence when they work alongside leaders in more formal senior roles. Further detail on the project can be found in the 'Research Use in Schools' section of the Education Endowment Foundation's website (http://educationendowmentfoundation.org.uk/).

The growth in social media such as Twitter and TeachMeets has enabled an expansion in opportunities for teachers and leaders to engage with and debate research and evidence (albeit with minimal quality control). A question for leaders is whether they are doing enough to encourage staff to engage in these opportunities and to evaluate the impact.

- **TAKE-OUT** ③: In larger schools or across partnerships, middle leaders can be vital catalysts for animating evidence in practice, but they need capacity and support from senior leaders if they are to succeed in this role (see *resource box 1.4*).

RESOURCE BOX 1.4:

Middle leaders are often dubbed the 'engine room of improvement', but this can leave them feeling trapped in their own schools, with few opportunities to connect and share their expert knowledge with other middle leaders and teachers, especially in other schools. Led by Professor Louise Stoll, the ESRC-funded Middle Leaders as Catalysts project has explored practical ways to address this, through the development of simple knowledge-exchange tools. The results will be published in 2015 (and further information can be found in Chapter 5).

The Harris Federation in London is offering the IOE's Leading Research and Development Within and Across Schools module as part of its school-based master's in leadership as a way to build the capacity of middle leaders in this area. Further detail on the module, led by Dr Chris Brown, can be found in the 'study' section of the IOE's website (www.ioe.ac.uk/study).

- **TAKE-OUT** ④: Professional learning must be collaborative, challenging, sustained, and supported. When it comes to evidence use, professional learning must also involve co-creation – bringing together knowledge from practice and knowledge from research to create knowledge that is new to everyone in the room (see *resource box 1.5*).

RESOURCE BOX 1.5:

The WANDLE alliance in London has invited all staff from across six participating secondary schools to join themed Joint Practice Development Groups. These are facilitated by trained school staff who are given research resources as a starting point for development work in their groups. Further detail can be found in the 'teaching school' section of Chesterton Primary School's website (www.chesterton.wandsworth.sch.uk/).

The Woodroffe Teaching School in Dorset offers a professional masters programme to staff across the alliance in partnership with Bath Spa University. The alliance also has its own CPD programme and supports teachers from different schools to work in groups of three using a Lesson Study format supported by a Specialist Leader of Education (SLE). Further detail can be found in the report *How Teaching Schools are Making a Difference: Part 2*, which is available in the 'publications' section of www.gov.uk: www.gov.uk/government/uploads/system/uploads/attachment_data/file/330579/how-teaching-schools-are-making-a-difference-part-2.pdf.

- **TAKE-OUT** ⑤: School–university partnerships can support much of this work, but most are weak due to issues of culture and capacity. Successful partnerships depend on local leaders who can create a 'third space', which gets the best from research and practice (see *resource box 1.6*).

Resource box 1.6:

Black and Wiliam's 'black box' (1998) research on formative assessment was founded on a comprehensive review of evidence, but this was then tested and developed through action research with schools in Medway and Oxfordshire to identify practical implementation strategies. See: www.oecd.org/edu/ceri/34260938.pdf.

A number of school–university research networks and partnerships exist to enable similar work, such as at Manchester, Cambridge, Winchester/Expansive Education, and the UCL Institute of Education. There are also non-university partnerships, such as the National Teacher Enquiry Network and Whole Education. See: *School–University Partnerships: Fulfilling the Potential, Summary Report*, by T. Greany, Q. Gu, G. Handscomb, and M. Varley, NCCPE, forthcoming, and the IOE's R&D network: www.ioe-rdnetwork.com/.

- **TAKE-OUT** ⑥: Policy and funding have a significant role to play in creating an enabling framework for evidence-informed practice. Key roles include: ensuring coherence, quality, and a focus on public engagement in research-commissioning programmes; ensuring research is accessible and quality assured; and building capacity and demand within and across schools (see *resource box 1.7*).

RESOURCE BOX 1.7:

Some of these roles and activities are already partly in place, for example through the Education Endowment Foundation's Pupil Premium/ Teaching and Learning Toolkit (see the 'Teaching and Learning Toolkit' section of the EEF's website: http://educationendowmentfoundation. org.uk/toolkit).

The Labour Party has called for an Office for Educational Improvement, which would provide independent advice on reform strategies, potentially building on the What Works Centre role currently played by the Education Endowment Foundation (see the 'What Works Network' of the EEF's website: (http://educationendowmentfoundation. org.uk/about/what-works-network/).

Chapter appendix

Recent and ongoing LCLL knowledge mobilization studies that have informed the take-out message claims are set out in Table 1.1.

Table 1.1: Recent and ongoing LCLL knowledge mobilization studies

Name and funder	Summary	Research team	Timescale
Middle leaders as catalysts for improving teacher practice: developing a knowledge exchange and impact network with Challenge Partner schools	Established and supported a network of middle leaders across Challenge Partner schools, who then extended their learning to their partner schools.	Professor Louise Stoll, Dr Chris Brown, Karen Spence-Thomas, and Carol Taylor	2013–14
	A parallel evaluation sought to assess the impact on knowledge sharing between schools.	London Centre for Leadership in Learning, UCL Institute of Education, with Challenge Partners	
ESRC Knowledge Exchange Opportunities Scheme			

Name and funder	Summary	Research team	Timescale
R&D themes research on great pedagogy and great CPD with Teaching Schools Additional research into how teaching schools are developing their R&D approaches National College for Teaching and Leadership (NCTL)	The teaching schools network agreed three national themes as the focus of their research activities for 2012–14: 1. What makes great pedagogy? 2. What makes great professional development that leads to consistently great pedagogy? 3. How can leaders lead successful teaching school alliances that enable the development of consistently great pedagogy? The IOE and Sheffield Hallam University (SHU) have supported 66 TSAs to undertake R&D under themes 1 and 2. An initial literature review on each theme was shared and a logic model developed to underpin the project. Alliances have used the Connecting Professional Learning methodology (Harris and Jones, 2012) and reported progress and findings using the framework. Early in 2014, funding from NCTL enabled the IOE/ SHU team to undertake additional case studies and a survey to investigate how TSAs are developing their R&D approach. Reports from both strands will be published in early 2015.	UCL Institute of Education (IOE) and Sheffield Hallam University (SHU)	2012–14

Name and funder	Summary	Research team	Timescale
School–university partnership learning initiative Research Councils UK and the National Co-ordinating Centre for Public Engagement	The school–university partnership learning initiative was commissioned to inform the potential for an ongoing programme of work aimed at enhancing the quality and impact of school–university partnerships. The project involved a literature review; a series of semi-structured interviews; a survey of universities, schools, funding bodies, the third sector, professional bodies/learned societies, and policymakers; and a project workshop.	Toby Greany (IOE), Qing Gu (Nottingham University), Graham Handscomb (independent) and Matt Varley (Nottingham Trent University)	2014
Evaluation of DfE's approach to developing evidence-based practice (with Sheffield Hallam University and Durham University)	The DfE has developed a logic model within which it has started to take action to improve the system of evidence-based teaching. The evaluation will track progress towards a system within which the teaching profession can improve practice through the rigorous use of robust evidence, and the DfE's role in facilitating the process. The evaluation will include a live evidence review, content analysis of policy and school-level documents, qualitative interviews, and the development of a matrix of engagement.	Toby Greany, Louise Stoll and Chris Brown (IOE), Mike Coldwell and Bronwen Maxwell (SHU), and Steve Higgins (Durham)	2014–16

Name and funder	Summary	Research team	Timescale
IOE R&D network www.ioe-rdnetwork.com/	The IOE R&D network aims to build on the Institute's existing research partnerships with schools to make them more sustainable and effective. The network was developed based on extensive consultation and prototyping with over 100 schools in 2013–14. It aims to build expertise and capacity for high-quality collaborative research and development. A series of core principles reflect a commitment to partnership, equity, and impact.	Led by Toby Greany and Karen Spence-Thomas on behalf of the IOE	Launched in 2014
Research Learning Communities Education Endowment Foundation	This project is exploring ways to build the capacity of primary schools to use evidence. It is working with an intervention group of 58 primary schools. A senior leader and 'evidence champion' from each school will work as part of a community of 5–6 schools to explore the evidence relating to an agreed improvement theme. They will come together for four workshops each year to examine the research and to develop, apply, and evaluate school improvement strategies which reflect this evidence.	Led by Dr Chris Brown, with Toby Greany, Louise Stoll, and a team from the IOE. The project will be evaluated by Bristol University as an RCT	2014–16

Endnotes

[1] The Office for Standards in Education (Ofsted) is England's school inspection body.

[2] School Direct gives successful schools responsibility for working with an accredited provider of teacher training to recruit trainees and shape their training experience. By 2014/15 almost half of all teacher training places in England were allocated via School Direct.

[3] The Coalition's 2010 white paper *The Importance of Teaching* (Department for Education, 2010) announced the intention to designate 500 outstanding schools as Teaching Schools that would lead initial and continuing professional development, school-to-school support, and research and development in partnership with an alliance of schools.

References

Black, P., and Wiliam, D. (1998) *Inside the Black Box: Raising standards through classroom assessment*. London: GL Assessment.

Brown, C., and Rogers, S. (2014) 'Knowledge creation as an approach to facilitating evidence-informed practice: Examining ways to measure the success of using this method with early years practitioners in Camden (London)'. *Journal of Educational Change*, 16 (1), 79–99. Early online publication. http://link.springer.com/article/10.1007/s10833-014-9238-9 (accessed 19 January 2015; requires subscription).

Cordingley, P. (2013) *The Contribution of Research to Teachers' Professional Learning and Development*. Online. www.bera.ac.uk/wp-content/uploads/2013/12/BERA-Paper-5-Continuing-professional-development-and-learning.pdf (accessed 22 November 2014).

Department for Education (2010) *The Importance of Teaching: The schools white paper 2010*. London: The Stationery Office. Online. www.education.gov.uk/schools/toolsandinitiatives/schoolswhitepaper/b0068570/the-importance-of-teaching (accessed 13 August 2013).

Earley, P., Higham, R., Allen, R., Allen, T., Howson, J., Nelson, R., Rawar, S., Lynch, S., Morton, L., Mehta, P., and Sims, D. (2012) *Review of the School Leadership Landscape*. Nottingham: National College for School Leadership.

Freedman, S., Lipson, B., and Hargreaves, D. (2008) *More Good Teachers*. London: Policy Exchange.

Godfrey, D. (2014) 'Creating a research culture: Lessons from other schools'. Online. www.sec-ed.co.uk/best-practice/creating-a-research-culture-lessons-from-other-schools (accessed 22 November 2014).

Goldacre, B. (2013) *Building Evidence into Education*. London: Department for Education. Online. http://media.education.gov.uk/assets/files/pdf/b/ben%20goldacre%20paper.pdf (accessed 25 January 2015).

Gough, D. (2013) 'Knowledge mobilisation in education in England'. In Levin, B., Qi, J., Edelstein, H., and Sohn, J. (eds) *The Impact of Research in Education: An international perspective*. Bristol: Policy Press, 65–84.

Greany, T. (2014) *Are We Nearly There Yet?: Progress, issues, and possible next steps for a self-improving school system*. London: Institute of Education Press.

Gu, Q., Rea, S., Hill, R., Smethem, L., and Dunford, J. (2014) *Teaching Schools Evaluation: Emerging issues from the early development of case study teaching school alliances – DfE research report*. Nottingham: National College for Teaching and Leadership.

Handscomb, G., and MacBeath, J. (2003) *The Research-Engaged School*. Colchester: Essex County Council, Forum for Learning and Research Enquiry (FLARE).

Hargreaves, D. (1996) *The Teacher Training Agency Annual Lecture 1996: Teaching as a Research-Based Profession: Possibilities and prospects*. Online. http://eppi.ioe.ac.uk/cms/Portals/0/PDF%20reviews%20and%20summaries/ TTA%20Hargreaves%20lecture.pdf (accessed 14 January 2013).

Harris, A., and Jones, M. (2012) 'Connect to learn: Learn to connect'. *Professional Development Today*, 14 (4), 13–19.

Hemsley-Brown, J. (2005) 'Using research to support management decision making within the field of education'. *Management Decision*, 43 (5), 691–705.

Higgins, S., Wall, K., Baumfield, V., Hall, E., Leat, D., Moseley, D., and Woolner, P. (2007) *Learning to Learn in Schools Phase 3 Evaluation: Technical appendices to the final report*. Online. http://campaign-for-learning.org.uk/cfl/ assets/documents/Research/L2LPhase3TechnicalAppendices.pdf (accessed 22 November 2014).

Levin, B. (2013) 'To know is not enough: Research knowledge and its use'. *Review of Education*, 1 (1), 2–31.

Levin, B., Cooper, A., Arjomand, S., and Thompson, K. (2011) 'Can simple interventions increase research use in secondary schools?' *Canadian Journal of Educational Administration and Policy*, 126 (5 December), 1–29.

Levin, B., Qi, J., Edelstein, H., and Sohn, J. (eds) (2013) *The Impact of Research in Education: An international perspective*. Bristol: Policy Press.

McLaughlin, C., Black-Hawkins, K., and McIntyre, D. (2004) *Researching Teachers, Researching Schools, Researching Networks: A review of the literature*. Cambridge: University of Cambridge.

Matthews, P., and Berwick, G. (2013) *Teaching Schools: First among equals*. Online. www.gov.uk/government/uploads/system/uploads/attachment_data/ file/329742/teaching-schools-first-among-equals.pdf (accessed 19 January 2015).

Matthews, P., and Hill, R. (2008) *Schools Leading Schools: The power and potential of National Leaders of Education*. Nottingham: National College for School Leadership.

— (2010) *Schools Leading Schools II: The growing impact of National Leaders of Education*. Nottingham: National College for Leadership of Schools and Children's Services.

Micklewright, J., Jerrim, J., Vignoles, A., Jenkins, A., Allen, R., Ilie, S., Bellarbre, E., Barrera, F., and Hein, C. (2014) *Teachers in England's Secondary Schools: Evidence from TALIS 2013 research report*. London: Department for Education/Institute of Education.

Mincu, M. (2014) 'Inquiry paper 6: Teacher quality and school improvement: What is the role of research?' In The British Educational Research Association/ The Royal Society for the Encouragement of the Arts, Manufacturing and Commerce, *The Role Of Research in Teacher Education: Reviewing the evidence*, 28–34. Online. www.bera.ac.uk/wp-content/uploads/2014/02/BERA-RSA-Interim-Report.pdf (accessed 8 November 2014).

National Teacher Research Panel Survey (2011) *Habitats for Teacher Research: Teacher perspectives on research as a sustainable environment for CPD*. Online. www.ntrp.org.uk/sites/all/documents/NTRP%20survey%20report%20 FINAL_0.pdf (accessed 29 January 2015).

Nelson, J., and O'Beirne, C. (2014) *Using Evidence in the Classroom: What works and why?* Slough: National Foundation for Educational Research.

Nutley, S., Powell, A., and Davies, H. (2013) *What Counts as Good Evidence?: Provocation paper for the Alliance for Useful Evidence.* Online. www.alliance4usefulevidence.org/assets/What-Counts-as-Good-Evidence-WEB.pdf (accessed 8 November 2014).

Nutley, S., Walter, I., and Davies, H. (2007) *Using Evidence: How research can inform public services.* Bristol: Policy Press.

Rycroft-Malone, J. (2008) 'Evidence-informed practice: From individual to context'. *Journal of Nursing Management*, 16 (4), 404–8.

Sandals, L., and Bryant, B. (2014) *The Evolving Education System in England: A 'temperature check'.* London: Department for Education.

Sharp, C., Eames, A., Sanders, D., and Tomlinson, K. (2006) *Leading a Research-Engaged School.* Nottingham: National College for School Leadership.

Stoll, L. (2008) 'Leadership and policy learning communities: Promoting knowledge animation'. In Chakroun, B., and Sahlberg, P. (eds) European Training Foundation Yearbook 2008: *Policy learning in action.* Luxembourg: European Training Foundation/Office for Official Publications of the European Communities, 107–12.

Thomas, G., and Pring, R. (eds) (2004) *Evidence-Based Practice in Education.* Maidenhead: Open University Press.

Waldegrave, H., and Simons, J. (2014) *Watching the Watchmen: The future of school inspections in England.* London: Policy Exchange.

Chapter 2

Evidence and quality

Tom Bennett

Chapter overview

In this chapter I look at notions of quality in relation to educational evidence. I begin by exploring how our understanding of what good evidence is has evolved from a very scientific perspective. This evolution has a number of implications for how teachers and policymakers have traditionally come to understand the 'use-value' and 'rigour' of research. Yet these implications can be challenged, and I examine the extent and scope of all forms of knowledge to contribute meaningfully to practice in the classroom, with an emphasis on the limitations of both quantitative and qualitative methods, and a discussion of where each can be most powerful. I then suggest what should count as good research from a teacher's point of view and explore common pitfalls that can trick the unwary: for example, advocacy disguised as objectivity, research published to serve political interests, and research published through non-standard routes.

Connecting research to practice

There is a peculiar dislocation between education research and research practice. On one hand are the factories of academia, churning out paper after paper; on the other, teachers in classrooms. But when do these magisteria traditionally overlap? Experience has shown me the answer is, with notable exceptions, 'infrequently', at least systematically. The experience most teachers have with research is at best a distant one: the PGCE student who, as part of his or her professional studies meets Vygotsky, Dewey, or Wiliam as part of a set task or set reading. This is then swallowed, like an enormous jawbreaker, and absorbed subconsciously for the rest of the teacher's career, neither challenged nor supplemented over time. Alternatively, teachers may find themselves less explicitly directed by research, in a manner that echoes Keynes's (1965) claim that the most practical man, who feels himself free from ideology, is in actual fact in the grip of the ideas of some long-dead economist. As Žižek (1989) states, it is when we feel ourselves to be the least in the grip of ideology, that we are most completely within its grasp.

This subliminal influence emerges from the assumptions and prejudices of the cradle of the teacher's career – the mentors, tutors, colleagues, and line management. It emerges also from the baggage that we bring from our own experiences of school. There are many working in education who, presented with this piece of research or that, will confidently exclaim that the findings are 'obvious', that is to say intuitively demonstrable by Descartes' 'clear light of reason'. But this is instantly given the lie by any practitioner for whom the axiom in question is not only not intuitively obvious, but can be refuted with vigour. And the institutions that generate most formal research – the think tanks, the universities, the education intermediaries, corporate bodies, and quangos, often find the gulf between laboratory and classroom too great to bridge. How many papers and studies fall from the nest and form a mulch at the foot of the tree where they were born? How many library shelves groan with bound volumes of unread journals?

This picture is obviously a caricature, but only just. There are avenues between these poles that enjoy healthy traffic, but they are few and far between. Why has this relationship developed in such a way? It would be difficult to imagine a similar dislocation existing between, for example, the field of metallurgy and its practical application in the world of aviation. And it would be impossible to countenance a mobile phone industry that did not depend upon the study of electromagnetic radiation and field theory.

The answer rests upon a profound dissimilarity that exists between the study of education and the study of such arenas as physics and chemistry: what constitutes evidence? More than that, it involves the history and evolution of these different areas, and an understanding – or perhaps a misunderstanding – of what the scientific method involves. Finally, it falls to the difference in the ways in which this evidence is verified. In the rest of this chapter I will explore all three aspects of what evidence means in education, as well as suggest ways in which we can avoid the problems associated with understanding the differences.

The history of science, and social science

Until the twentieth century, science did not exist. That is to say it existed, but no one called it that. Instead, our ancestors knew it as natural philosophy. At its heart lay a simple but profound idea: we learn more about the universe and the world around us by observing it, recording those observations, and then trying to make sense of it all. While that may seem deeply unimpressive, it was a huge leap. Of course this was the way in which people tried to understand the world in their everyday lives, but it was haphazard and subject to personal bias and prejudice. It was also contested by a long tradition of what we now call rationalism – the philosophy that the best bases on which to make knowledge claims about anything were reason and introspection. To be fair, rationalism also had justification for claiming efficacy; mathematics, for example, was as close to pure reason and logic as it was possible to imagine, and its formulae seemed to apply to the external world as well as working on paper.

Science came about as a formalization of the 'watch it and work it out method', which came to be known as empiricism (from *empeiros*, meaning 'experience'). And from that we obtain the empirical method of science: experience.

What is empirical science?

Science has many features, but several are core, and are sufficient to define the concept in ways even the layperson can grasp without risk of serious error:

- Observation. The participant in empirical science begins with an observation, or series of observations, about the world, recorded with as little prejudice as possible. Instead of saying 'I saw an angel' the recorder writes 'I saw a bright light in the sky which lasted for thirteen seconds'. The observation must be interpreted as little as possible.
- A hypothesis. The observer then suggests a hypothesis as to why the observed phenomena have occurred. For example: you might notice that water boils and becomes a gas at certain times. When? It is observed that it tends to happen whenever it is placed above something producing heat, such as a fire or a stove. This might lead one to speculate that heat by itself will turn water to steam. Of course, it might not be that; perhaps stoves alone, cold or hot, will do the same. Perhaps the desire for tea boils water; perhaps the light from the fire. I'm labouring this point, but only for clarity.
- Design a test. The observer designs an experiment which will test the hypothesis, for example that heat boils water. The test might be to apply heat to the water at different temperatures to see which ones result in steam and which do not. The test can then be carried out at different heights, times of day, using different materials, and so on. All the data are recorded.
- Analyse the data. What has been found? Are there any consistencies in the observations? Just as importantly, can the observations be explained in any other way? What problems were encountered in the experiment? Could the theory be wrong in other ways?

- Come to a conclusion. You might conclude that heat is the most significant variable in the production of steam. You might speculate that pressure has an effect. You test the theory again. You publish results. Crucially, you allow others to examine your data and work to see what conclusions they come up with – peer review – allowing others to attempt to disprove or support your experimental data by repetition. By now you can claim to be involved in science.

These factors are crucial. By insisting on replicability, you strengthen the claims that your theory holds true either universally, or at least in multiple contexts. If it does not, you investigate why not. By attempting falsification, you armour yourself against the possibility that you are forming inappropriate conclusions about your own evidence, or simply reinforcing your prejudices. By allowing peer review, you accelerate that process.

Empirical science requires these fundamental premises: that the physical universe operates on regular and – in theory – predictable principles that are not chaotic, and are not subject to the whim of some universal spirit. (This used to be called natural law: God preferred his creation to operate in a regular fashion, but it was still subject to his convenience, and therefore malleable to his will.) In other words, the speed of light in Romford is the same as the speed of light in Bombay, and if it is not, it will be because of another universal principle, such as gravity, that is itself regular. Empirical science assumes the existence of a universe external to our minds. It assumes that there exists a reality where matter also exists, which is not subject to mental relativity. In other words, if a tree falls in a forest and no one is there to hear it, it might not make a sound (which we might call a social construct) but it certainly suggests that matter oscillated at a certain frequency that we would associate with the experience of sound. Philosophically we can call this Realism.

Science and social science

After the successes of physics, chemistry, and the other physical sciences, wise men and women attempted to turn this approach to the world of humanity. The benefit and mastery brought about by the scientific revolution was an enormously attractive prize for the social sphere. Economics, politics, and later sociology, psychology, criminology, and a host of variants, all attempted to systematize and build upon the scientific method of analysis. Unfortunately, while this succeeded in creating new models where knowledge and analysis could be shared, accumulated, and built upon, it failed to achieve the cumulative efficacy enjoyed by the physical sciences. Why? There are several reasons:

- Human action is far less predictable than the relatively reliable behaviour of matter.
- It is also subject to a vast array of possible causal factors. The density of these potential causes makes it extremely difficult to differentiate between them; not impossible, merely difficult.
- What causes one human behaviour may cause a completely different behaviour at another time. Simple causal relationships between, for example, reasons and actions are often hard to construe accurately.

And these considerations are preceded by other philosophical considerations of even greater difficulty, such as notions of free will or gaps in universal causality. It is far from obvious that human action is predicated on deterministic grounds, in which case attempts to draw testable conclusions and universal theories are doomed. But in the absence of certainty – which, after all, is not to be found even in the natural sciences – there may be some solace in probability.

Quantitative and qualitative evidence

The strength of the natural sciences has been their ability to lend themselves to quantitative analysis: the objects of their examination are amenable to being counted, measured, and weighed. Anything with a numerical quotient is easily comparable. If you want to know which metal will make the best fireguard, simply heat up two samples and take the temperature at which both fail, for example. That experiment can then be repeated, shared with others, and tested. The data captured can be applied equally from Bearsden to Bangladesh. It is far easier for people to agree on the outcomes of experimentation when it can be comparatively assessed using the unarguable yardstick of numbers. It is hard to challenge the claim that the Empire State Building is taller than the Hoover Dam when every measuring tape supports it, unless you want to argue the paradox that two is less than one.

The problem for the social sciences (and educational research) is that so often what we want to investigate cannot be reduced to numbers. When Jeremy Bentham produced his hedonic calculus, a method by which pleasures could be measured and compared with one another, even his attempts at reduction failed. The duration of a pleasure could probably be measured. But its intensity? Its propinquity? Such matters are abstract concepts that exist as secondary properties in the mind of the one experiencing them. Temperature is absolute, but *hot* and *cold* are not. The frequency of the notes in a Beethoven movement can be described numerically, but the sound cannot. The experienced human realm seems to be constructed of unquantifiable intangibles that we understand but cannot describe numerically because they are not intuitively quantifiable. Instead they are qualitative experiences. It might even be argued that the majority of what we experience consciously is comprised of these types of experience. Typically we only experience numbers in a very intuitive manner in our everyday lives.

Evidence is frequently divided into two realms: quantitative – that which can be numbered – and qualitative – that which can be expressed only in qualities. Both are important forms of evidence; both are necessary to understand as closely as possible the phenomena you wish to investigate. If you wanted to research, for example, the impact of serving in the armed forces, you could capture data that expressed the number of soldiers that received counselling, suicide rates, crime rates, and so on. You could then undertake statistical analysis with this data and seek interesting patterns between seemingly random events. Or, you could interview the participants and ask them to describe their experiences, making case studies of their responses that could then fuel a qualitative analysis, where the researcher's skill in evaluation would be paramount.

Both approaches have value; both have strengths, and both have perils. The quantitative approach enjoys robust comparative powers; is far more easily reproduced (or not) by repetition; and approaches indisputability, at least in the bare facts (that is, it is far more amenable to being shown to be the case, or not the case). The limitation is that such data fail to capture the lived experience of the object of investigation. In the case of the veterans above, a quantitative analysis of their experiences would obviously be incomplete for any serious student of, for example, post-traumatic stress disorders.

So too in education, where so much of what we seek to understand is comprised of the lived experience of its participants. So many of the questions we ask in this arena are related to unquantifiables: what constitutes literacy? How valuable is this essay compared with another in this book? It is clear that the realm of subjectivity is an important part of understanding education.

The dangers of educational research
This, however, does not lead us inevitably towards the conclusion that all qualitative data is equally valuable, just as we must avoid the mistake

of thinking that quantifiable data is the only important prize to obtain. Throughout the whole of its existence, the field of education has been subject to dubious practices and assuredly bad science. To be fair, no field of science is immune to these syndromes, and many sins are committed in the name of commercial or reputational gain, resulting in tortured science, prejudiced analysis, ridiculously enthusiastic conclusions, and at times plain deceit and invention.

But at least in the natural sciences, such devices can, to some extent, be verified or disproved. In the social sciences, and in education, it is possible to find research that makes claims of efficacy that are unsupported in any way that can be proven or not. For example, many practitioners claim that role play is a powerful tool for improving the learning experience of students; or, if not role play, substitute discovery learning, or using Thinking Hats, or Multiple Intelligence theory. The difficulty arises when we attempt to establish if the interventions had the effects claimed. And we find that qualitative data proves to be a mercurial subject. In my own investigation to find a solid evidence base to support many of the claims of the IT-adoption communities, for example, I found a large number of testimonials and enthusiastic case studies from participants based on, for example, satisfaction surveys and feedback forms, but very little hard evidence of impact.

Of course, the feelings of the participants are not insignificant indicators of impact. And as far as evidence goes, it is incontestable that a great deal of the development of what I regard as expertise in teaching is generated by reflective experience – the craft and art of teaching one might say. This is problematic in two ways. First, it is vulnerable to the prejudices and assumptions of the teacher, who may be willing their interventions to have the impact they desire, and second it provides very little impetus for the intervention to be adopted by anyone else. If I want to convince a friend to buy a car, and I know that he likes fast cars, I can refer to the power of the engine and the ceiling on the speedometer. But if I recommend a restaurant because 'I had the best time there', then caveat emptor.

This is especially important in the field of education for two reasons:

- Cost: everything that happens in a school costs money. Some interventions, for example iPad adoption, can be enormously expensive. But the evidence base for their efficacy simply does not exist yet. That is not to say they are not a tremendous boon to learning (perhaps they are) but the data we have does not support this conclusion yet. And as interventions go, they are not inexpensive.

- Opportunity Cost: everything done in a school is done within the context of finite time, attention, and administration. Therefore everything done in a school that has no effect detracts from interventions that could have an impact. When it comes to a commodity as precious as minutes of a child's life that cannot be regained, especially a poor child's life for whom education might be the last vehicle of social mobility available, this is a grave responsibility.

We can see that no form of evidence is intrinsically bad or good – it merely carries within itself intrinsic strengths and weaknesses and, as long as these are borne in mind, by itself no data – if it is honestly harvested – can be dangerous. Quantitative data is powerfully comparable, and lends itself to statistical analysis. However, it is wise to remember that statistical analysis is no layperson's field; it requires training in its language to avoid making non-intuitive errors. Similarly, qualitative data (again, gathered with integrity) can possess reservoirs of meaning and value, but must always be understood as contextual, subjective, and often profoundly relativistic. Sometimes one form of evidence is powerful in understanding a given subject, sometimes another. A healthy awareness of these limitations and powers is essential for the appreciation of the limits and utility of any evidence we encounter. Randomized controlled trials (RCTs), for example, have become a popular way of assessing the overall efficacy of many interventions. The strength of such a method is that it provides an often useful, global, and holistic view of the direction in which enormous amounts of data might be pointing. The weakness is that it frequently steamrollers over the more subtle, granular aspects of the data.

Is social science a science?

Many argue that social science is not science. They claim that social science fails to meet the exacting standards of the natural sciences because it is unable to provide adequate controls, because participants are frequently aware of the interventions they receive, and because human beings are so resistant to universal predictive claims. This may lead us to conclude that just as a false god is not actually a god, a social science is not a science. Certainly some appalling crimes against education have been justified in the name of science, while having little actually to do with it. For examples see *resource box 2.1.*

There is a long list of previously or currently popular fashions in education that have all been justified on the basis of bad, limited, or absent evidence bases. In other situations, good research has been subverted by the political desires and needs of the classroom or the school leadership hierarchy: assessment for learning, for example, which was the result of Black and Wiliam's meta-study *Inside the Black Box* (1998), but which was quickly misadopted by schools as a box-ticking exercise in administrative legerdemain rather than as its architects imagined it. This legacy of weak, fraudulent, misappropriated, and biased evidence bases must be considered by policymakers, schools, and teachers as much as time and finances permit, in order to avoid repeating the policy mistakes of the past.

RESOURCE BOX 2.1:

Non-scientific education interventions:

Brain Gym: The poster child of this syndrome, this now-discredited intervention claimed that students should rub 'brain buttons' (basically acupressure points) and drink water 'through the roof of your mouth' (for rapid absorption, allegedly). It raged fashionably throughout thousands of schools. The fire has largely gone out, but it is still found in remote pockets. While it is not widely adopted any more, it provides us with a case study in how rapidly snake oil can infect an unprepared host. This is why it is important for schools and teachers to be as research literate as possible, and to ask for the evidence that underpins every claim made.

Learning Styles: The belief that everyone learns differently, because their brains are hardwired to learn visually or kinaesthetically for example, has now been fairly comprehensively demonstrated to be unproven. Note, not proven untrue, merely unproven. Not only does it lack a legitimate evidence base as a working model of learning, not only is current thinking about how the mind works at odds with its premises, but no demonstrable impact has been discovered by utilizing learning styles as a learning tool. Yet it persists, and is widely adopted.

Multiple Intelligences: This is another popular theory, which is again unsupported by an evidence base. The division of intelligences into an apparently arbitrary taxonomy has little to recommend it. It lingers, as many of these theories do, because it appeals to the tastes of the listener.

Flipped Learning: This fashionable orthodoxy has proven popular with early adopters of digital classrooms, but as yet has very little evidence to demonstrate efficacy. This has not prevented enormous sums of money from being spent promoting its benefits, often by commercial interests directly profiting from its promotion. Again, this is not to deny the possibility of its utility, nor to cast aspersions on those who promote its use.

Conclusion

There are many sources of evidence available to everyone in the teaching community. A healthy appreciation of their limitations is key to avoiding falling into the traps of naivety and cognitive bias. And an equally healthy appreciation of their possibilities can open avenues of benefit, safe from the impediment of dogma and cant. The exciting possibility is that we now exist in an age when communication and information technology has made it possible for us to appreciate both.

Take-out messages

- **TAKE-OUT** ①: Whenever a school is deciding how to allocate its budgets; whenever a teacher is designing a lesson, or a curriculum; whenever anyone in education makes a decision, they need to consider upon what evidence their decision rests.
- **TAKE-OUT** ②: Not all evidence is good evidence (and not all claimed evidence necessarily exists): there is a long list of previously or currently popular fashions in education that have been justified on the basis of bad, limited, or absent evidence bases.
- **TAKE-OUT** ③: Correspondingly, a critical appreciation of forms of evidence and how they were produced is key to avoiding falling into the traps of naivety and cognitive bias.
- **TAKE-OUT** ④: Teachers' experience (and the experience of others whom we trust such as mentors, coaches, and trainers) is an important source of our judgements and knowledge, and is not to be dismissed, as long as we are alert to the possibility that our experiences may be clouded by partiality and prejudice, and that our human sense of scale is often too frail to appreciate a macro-world.

References

Black, P., and Wiliam, D. (1998) *Inside the Black Box: Raising standards through classroom assessment*. London: GL Assessment.

Keynes, J.M. (1965) *The General Theory of Employment, Interest and Money*. Basingstoke: Palgrave Macmillan.

Žižek, S. (1989) *The Sublime Object of Ideology*. London: Verso.

Chapter 3

'Evidence' and teaching: A question of trust?

Lesley Saunders

Chapter overview

This chapter questions the notion of 'evidence' as a basis for teachers' professional knowledge, on the grounds that 'evidence' is problematic for technical, practical, and ethical reasons. It proposes instead a three-fold metaphor – the 'art, craft, and science of pedagogy' – for understanding and articulating the depth and complexity of what teachers know, believe, and do. The chapter briefly reminds readers of the decade or more of 'evidence-based education' under a previous government. One of the key lessons from that work is the need to have a broader conceptualization of the role of research and scholarship in teaching, one that should be integral to the initial and continuing education of teachers. Given the absence of a sustainable strategy for embedding research into the daily work of teaching, however, the chapter calls for requisite levels of funding and other resources to make research-informed practice feasible in reality as well as appealing in principle.

Evidence

'Evidence' is a policy fantasy that comes and goes; much like the exhortation that education can and must better meet the needs of industry and commerce, the call for teaching to be more evidence-based is perennial and seductive. And wrong.

Firstly, there is the technical issue of quality – of 'rigour' and 'robustness', in today's parlance. Despite the optimistic assessments of commentators like Goldacre (2013), Petty (2009), Slavin and colleagues at the Institute for Effective Education, and the Evidence-Based Teachers Network, this is more problematic than we might have hoped. Even in the field of medical science – so often held up as the ideal to which education and teaching should aspire – 'there is increasing concern that most current published research findings are false' (Ioannidis, 2005). That should make us all pause for further thought and reflection, not only about issues of individual study design, analysis, and reporting (including the prevailing idea that randomized controlled trials are the gold standard of research methods

– see, for example, Haynes *et al.*, 2012), but also about system issues such as publication bias, the red herring of citation data, and increasing competitive and commercial drivers. Evidence is not all it seems.

Secondly, in the sphere of education there are other kinds of consideration that are at least as important as the technical ones. There are the challenging practicalities for teachers of engaging in and with research – I have more to say on this later. And crucially there is the evergreen question of whether and how far a scientific notion of 'evidence' holds good in *educational* research. If, as Broadfoot (1988: 4) urged, 'educational research … occupies an uneasy conceptual and methodological middle ground between naturalistic science on the one hand and interpretive disciplines such as history and literature on the other', then we must decide not between these contrasting paradigms, but how to live with the right amount and kind of uncertainty.

A bit of history

Although we are often told that the twenty-first century is uniquely a knowledge-based society, the idea that knowledge, systematically gathered and widely disseminated, should inform decision making can be traced back a considerable way. Just one example: an 1894 report written for the government Board of Education argued that education would benefit from 'a well equipped educational intelligence office' (cited in Griffiths, 2003). Moving forward a century or so, 'evidence' in its millennial avatar was, fittingly, meant to signal the end of ideology as the key determinant of political decision making. (Key publications on 'evidence-based education' include Hargreaves, 1996; Hillage *et al.*, 1998; Davies, 1999; Davies *et al.*, 2000.) Famously, David Blunkett, then Secretary of State for Education, made an appeal to the research community to find out 'what works' (Blunkett, 2000: 12).

Although the phrase is barely more than a cliché now, then it sounded bracing and persuasive. And with the rhetoric came a large injection of government and other funding:

- as well as allocating a generous budget for contracted research – £139 million per annum by the mid-2000s – the Department for Education and Skills (DfES) invested in educational research in several other ways, including core funding for three dedicated thematic research centres, plus support for teachers through the Best Practice Research Scholarships scheme (see Furlong and Salisbury, 2005)
- the DfES also set up the National Educational Research Forum (NERF), whose purpose was to bring together researchers, practitioners, and policymakers to create a new national strategy that would transform

the system – a useful source of inside information on government-led educational research strategy during this period is White (2007)

- the Economic and Social Research Council (ESRC) funded the unprecedentedly large-scale, long-term Teaching and Learning Research Programme (TLRP) – see *resource box 3.1*

RESOURCE BOX 3.1:

TEACHING AND LEARNING RESEARCH PROGRAMME: www.tlrp. org/pub/

TLRP provides a number of useful resources, including:

- *Commentaries* – accessible, full-colour documents drawing evidence from a number of TLRP projects to comment on a particular topic. There are 15 briefings currently available, which can be downloaded free of charge.
- *Research briefings* – concise four-page summaries of findings. These are the best introductions to the work of individual TLRP projects. There are 70 briefings currently available and they can be downloaded free of charge.

- new levels of research synthesis and dissemination activity resulted in a plethora of websites, portals, online summaries, and so on, which often attempted to capture, categorize, and synthesize teachers' research alongside academic and contracted research – of particular note is the imaginative work of the Centre for Research and Evidence in Education (CUREE – see *resource box 3.2*)

RESOURCE BOX 3.2:

CENTRE FOR RESEARCH AND EVIDENCE IN EDUCATION: www. curee.co.uk

CUREE is an internationally acknowledged centre of expertise in evidence-based practice in all sectors of education. Led by Philippa Cordingley, CUREE staff use their knowledge and skills in teaching, research, communications, and knowledge management to produce high-quality research, CPD, and tools and resources. CUREE work with and for schools and colleges, academy chains, teaching schools and other clusters and alliances, and with professional associations, universities, and government departments and agencies in the UK and worldwide.

- the Teacher Training Agency (as it then was) established the groundbreaking school-based research consortia as well as the National Teacher Research Panel (see *resource box 3.3*)

RESOURCE BOX 3.3:

NATIONAL TEACHER RESEARCH PANEL: www.ntrp.org.uk

The National Teacher Research Panel was set up in 1999 to provide an expert teacher perspective to researchers, research funders, and policymakers on research priorities, projects, and reports. Since then, the panel has also worked to promote teaching as a research- and evidence-informed profession more broadly.

The panel has 15 members with significant expertise in teaching, in research, and in relating the two. All are practising teachers and tutors who are recruited via a challenging process that assesses their skills, knowledge, and suitability for the panel's work. Panel members are supported by a group of Specialist Advisers who provide additional research and subject expertise to support the panel's work.

- the National Foundation for Educational Research (NFER) established a model of the research-engaged school as a knowledge-creating community – see *resource box 3.4*.

RESOURCE BOX 3.4:

NATIONAL FOUNDATION FOR EDUCATIONAL RESEARCH RESEARCH MARK: www.nfer.ac.uk/schools/research-mark/

'Get recognition for your school's achievements in research'. NFER's 'Research Mark' scheme looks at what stage of research engagement schools are at: 'emerging', 'established', or 'extended'. It is based on ten criteria that NFER suggest are essential elements of a research-engaged school or college and includes a school visit by an NFER research associate who will give feedback, recommendations, and a full diagnostic report.

So no one can claim with any credibility that as a country we have not already invested substantially and over a ten-year period in the evidence-based education agenda. Yet we have to acknowledge that what is left from that decade is a residue rather than a proper legacy. A major casualty resulting from this is the lack of more nuanced ideas about the relationship between research and teaching in the Stenhousian tradition (see, for example, Rudduck and Hopkins, 1985; Thomas and Pring, 2004) by leading scholars like John Elliott, Michael Fielding, Hazel Hagger, Martyn Hammersley, Stephen Kemmis, Donald McIntyre, Richard Pring, Jean Rudduck, and Brian Simon (to name only a few).

The rest of this chapter addresses the implications of thinking about, and resourcing, teaching as a scholarly research-informed profession as distinct from an evidence-based set of behaviours. And this is at heart a question of what we think 'teaching' is – what analogies we draw, what metaphors we deploy, consciously or unconsciously – as well as of how we define 'research'.

Analogies and metaphors

At one point in her novel *Babel Tower*, A.S. Byatt has her main character think about thinking, about the heuristic process of enquiry; she has Marcus performing a sort of internal epistemological riff:

> [Marcus] thinks of his brain. He thinks of it as long powerful feathers curled in a skull shape, layer in layer. He thinks of this wordless thinking as preening, smoothing, until all the little hooks and eyes connect and the surface is glossy and brilliant. He does not know if this analogy is useful or misleading or both at once. He has begun to know enough about science to know that scientific thought moves along in such metaphors and analogies, *which it must both use and suspect.*
>
> (Byatt, 1997: 251, my emphasis)

We cannot avoid using analogy and metaphor when we talk about education, about teaching and learning, but we should use them with great caution. We should be aware of the resonances and undercurrents they bring with them; we should know their seductiveness as well as their limitations:

> I think there is a huge prize waiting to be claimed by teachers. By collecting better evidence about what works best, and establishing a culture where this evidence is used as a matter of routine, we can improve outcomes for children, and increase professional independence.
>
> This is not an unusual idea. Medicine has leapt forward with evidence based practice, because it's only by conducting 'randomized trials' – fair tests, comparing one treatment against another – that we've been able to find out what works

best. Outcomes for patients have improved as a result, through thousands of tiny steps forward.

(Goldacre, 2013: 7)

Goldacre – who has done immense public service through his newspaper column 'Bad Science' – is but the most recent government adviser to propose an analogy between medicine and teaching. Why cannot teachers be more like consultant surgeons, with a commitment to leading as well as utilizing the latest research in their treatment of patients? Or like GPs, with their computers open at the pages of the Cochrane Collaboration (www.cochrane.org) or the CPRD (Clinical Practice Research Datalink, www.cprd.com/intro.asp) as they prescribe patient treatments?

Why is there so much variation, and so little systematic innovation, in teaching practices across the country? The problem with this analogy is that teaching is not an 'intervention', a daily dosage downloaded from some lucrative big pharma. Teaching is one side of the coin of which the other is learning. Learning new and difficult things is what humans do, in just the way Byatt so wittily evokes. The child who asks a question and gets an answer that sooner or later provokes another question is doing something that is nothing like being a patient following a diet-sheet or swallowing prescription pills, and absolutely nothing like choosing between brand providers, purchasing a best buy. No, she is engaged in poking around, testing, puzzling, reflecting, being tantalized and stymied, proposing and rejecting explanations, stopping and starting; she is, to put it rather pompously, an agent of self-change.

So teaching is primarily the practice of relationships, albeit of a specific and specifiable kind called pedagogy, between people, with all that that entails about mutuality and meetings of minds, the centrality of emotions and ethics. The specifics of pedagogy also encompass professional knowledge, of course, meaning knowledge that is trustworthy and that – along with ethical conduct and public accountability – entitles teaching to claim to be a profession based on trust. Robin Alexander's definition of pedagogy is helpful here – it is:

> ... the act of teaching together with its attendant theory and discourse, which are collective, generalisable and open to public scrutiny. It is what one needs to know, and the skills one needs to command, in order to make and justify the many different kinds of decision of which teaching is constituted.

(Alexander, 2004: 11)

'The many different kinds of decision' – John Elliott had already alerted us to the irreducibly deliberative nature of teaching:

> It is not as if the moral ends are clear and all that is left is a decision about the most technically efficient means of satisfying them ... education [is] a morally complex affair involving a careful consideration of both the curriculum and pedagogy by teachers. From this perspective the quality of education depends on the quality of teachers' deliberation and judgement in the classroom.
>
> (Elliott, 1996: 218)

Consequently, Elliott argued, teaching is a transformational process deeply connected with the construction of knowledge through enquiry. Here, in a nutshell, is the expression of the intimate relationship between teaching and research: 'the structures of knowledge into which students are to be inducted are intrinsically problematic and contestable, and therefore objects of speculation', and so teachers can, and should, 'model [for their students] how to treat knowledge as an object of inquiry' (Elliott, 2001: 567).

Before saying a little more about research and teaching – 'research-informed teaching', 'research-in-teaching' – I want to suggest another analogy that I hope might one day turn out to be more than just a metaphor.

The 'art, craft, and science' of teaching

A challenge for anyone trying to analyse and articulate the complexities of pedagogy is to give full weight to the intuitive, improvised, and non-systematized aspects of teaching, while continuing to argue for the crucial importance of research and scholarship, the creation of those explicit, cumulative, and collective kinds of knowledge from which pedagogy derives its warrant.

While I was working at the General Teaching Council for England, we often talked about the 'art, craft, and science' of pedagogy (General Teaching Council, 2008). We argued that the 'art' of teaching lies in those holistic-tacit, in-the-moment, embodied, interpretative, performative, and relational aspects of teaching, manifested through countless interactions in every lesson. The 'craft' of teaching lies in the progressive acquisition of technical and contextualized practices that are mastered through a kind of apprenticeship, enacted in daily classroom routines, developed in particular settings, and more or less informally guided by experienced and expert colleagues. And the 'science' of teaching, we suggested, is the systematic acquisition and understanding of pedagogic strategies derived from cumulative research that is grounded in testable theory and open to scrutiny.

I think the analogy, the metaphors, hold true as far as they go, but they are only the basic groundwork for something far more ambitious: a collective way to talk about the complexity of pedagogy that is accessible to parents and the public as well as to teachers and academics. In a recent article for *Professional Development Today* (Saunders, 2014), I explored each of the metaphors in turn to see if they could yield anything a little more helpful. Briefly, if professional expertise is best understood not so much in terms of generic competences but as qualities, capacities, and dispositions that are subtle and situated, then a paradox arises: the further along the path from 'novice' to 'expert' a teacher travels, the less explicit and more second nature his/her practice becomes. That is why it is often a challenge for expert teachers to explain why they do what they do, and to articulate the precise reasons – ethical, emotional, intellectual – for the decisions they have made during any given lesson. But they do need to do this, not least so that novice teachers can incorporate 'the knowledge behind the practice' into their own understandings and behaviours. This is where the 'art', 'craft', and 'science' might come together, in teachers and academics working to develop innovative research methodologies that can successfully turn the fluent, tacit knowledge of expert teachers into more explicit, testable, and codifiable knowledge from which others can learn.

Even though I have to admit that this is a very provisional beginning and that combining the 'art', 'craft', and 'science' of teaching into a coherent and compelling account of pedagogy is more difficult than I had hoped, I am not convinced either that we can manage without such terminology. It seems to me to get close enough to the cognitive, affective, and embodied complexity of teaching to remain useful for the time being, until we have created a more nuanced, exact, and unifying description.

In any case, we probably should not want to dispense with metaphor entirely, even if we could. Metaphors invite us to question and explore, allowing us to acknowledge that there are some perceptions and experiences that go beyond our available conceptual categories. The art–craft–science metaphors also offer an ethical and aesthetic counterpoint to the martial language which has invaded education, with its battles against this and that, its aims, targets, strategies, and impact.

Research as enquiry

As readers may infer from what I have written so far, and as I have argued elsewhere (Saunders, 2010), I think there are two distinct ways of conceptualizing the role of research in education. One revolves around 'evidence', research as a kind of epistemic *product*, while the other foregrounds *the process* of enquiry, research as an activity.

Readers can perhaps appreciate how the former might be particularly relevant to the rhetoric and requirements of policymaking, while the latter fits very well with the deliberative nature of pedagogy and the need to exercise nuanced professional judgement in deciding between courses of action.

The 'process of enquiry' actually covers a range of different activities for teachers, such as:

- directly accessing research intelligence, for example through websites, reading groups, and researcher-in-school schemes, as well as journals and other media
- participating as active subjects in externally generated studies
- making a contribution to externally generated studies, for example by helping to collect and analyse data
- undertaking research as part of their accredited professional studies
- undertaking specific teacher-research activities outside accredited study
- actively experimenting in their own classroom using a reflective-evaluative enquiry approach
- working in pairs or groups to read, analyse, and discuss research relevant to professional and school development, and to design collaborative studies within or even across schools.

(Saunders, 2007: no page numbers)

As many writers have argued, research can offer teachers conceptual frameworks for thinking about a problem and tools for critical-reflective practice, as well as evaluations of pedagogic approaches that have been shown to be effective in similar contexts. McIntyre (2005) proposed that teachers need to be actively involved in critically trialling what he called 'research-based suggestions' as a means of creating authentic knowledge about teaching and learning. Brown and Rogers argue that engaging with research provides teachers with 'exposure to ideas and concepts [they] might not ordinarily come across' and that this exposure 'enhances the repertoire of "understanding"' (2014: 1). And in a thoughtful exploration of what research-informed practice entails, Lingard and Renshaw call for a 'researchly disposition' (2010: 27) to be instilled in teachers; they explicitly reject 'a model of teachers as simply translators or interpreters of educational research done elsewhere' and they defend a broad definition of educational research that encompasses research led and conducted by teachers.

Studies suggest that research-informed practice does indeed strengthen teachers' professional capacities; a recent systematic review of the field found that 'there is extensive evidence on links between engagement with and in research, and benefits for teachers' (Bell *et al.*, 2010: 33). But the obstacles to realizing this systemically have remained firmly in place despite the investments to which I referred before:

- *Inaccessibility of academic research as a resource for teachers.* Academic research continues to be written in a form and style that complies with university conventions, and is published through the medium of specialized journals whose numbers are vast and whose subscriptions are costly. So research that could be relevant to practice is inaccessible to the vast majority of teachers. The websites and portals listed above and in the resources can only do so much to re-cast, synthesize, and disseminate the vast amount of research that exists.

- *Time, opportunity, and priorities.* A common complaint by teachers is that there is insufficient time within an ordinary school day, week, or term to devote to activities that are not directly concerned with the immediate necessities of lesson planning, marking/assessment, and so on. Insufficient time to plan, construct, analyse, read, or otherwise engage with research has frequently been reported by teachers as an insuperable barrier.

- *Skills and knowledge.* Teachers also report a lack of skills and/or lack of confidence in research disciplines. These include the skills to make judgements on the quality of a piece of research in order to attach weight to its importance, and skills to 'activate' the research in their own context. Teachers very often feel they lack specific methodological skills to undertake research. However, the recent study by Brown and Rogers (2014) cited above gives some strong pointers as to how teachers' expertise in research use can be developed and enhanced.

Yet these may not be the primary obstacles. McIntyre (2005) has suggested that the gap between academic research and professional practice is actually a disjunction between two sharply contrasting kinds of knowledge. Here is a short example (taken from my personal experience) of how that gap might be bridged. A few years ago I helped to facilitate the process by which a small group of practitioners were trying to use the outcomes of a research review on the teaching of sustainable development to support and improve their practice in schools and environmental centres – the results of which were written up in Rickinson *et al.*, 2003. What I saw taught me that for some practitioners the form and language of research is a foreign one that they have to learn, and the practical application of what are often inconclusive findings presents them with an unfamiliar kind of intellectual struggle. Moreover, I saw that the researcher had to yield his expert and specialist ownership of the work in order to create the space for teachers to own their rather different meanings of it. This is an intense, messy, and tough process that must be understood in terms of professional development – adult pedagogy – and resourced accordingly.

I could also see that over time some of the teachers – who were initially united by their passion for the subject rather than by an interest in research – were starting to think about conducting small-scale research projects in their classrooms to test out or take further what the academic research was telling them. The project was genuinely an eye-opener for me: I could literally see and hear how research is a process that is collaborative, reflexive, and discursive. The knowledge created was of a kind that is comfortable with provisionality and that can make room for the contribution of the ethical and creative imagination as well as of rational cognition. Moreover, the research was not even primarily evidential, but was instrumental in getting people to question their assumptions. It clearly fulfilled what Engeström (2007) has called the capacity of research to 'evoke and support human agency'.

Conclusion

The relationship between research and practice is not straightforward, in education as in any other professional field. There is no simple formula by which academic researchers produce research evidence for teachers to use in their classrooms. To begin with, in our country a systemic separation between the worlds of schools and universities has led people to claim that 'researchers are lost in thought; practitioners are missing in action' (Desforges, 2009: 4). More fundamentally, the creation of expert professional knowledge is not a matter of 'applying' evidence designed and created elsewhere by others. It is a subtle combination of pre-service training and education, individual and collaborative learning through experience and critical reflection, and immersion in scholarly knowledge.

Two stark messages emerge from studies of research-informed practice: that teachers derive significant professional and pedagogic benefits from engaging in and with research; and that only a minority of teachers at any given time is thus engaged. Many teachers never undertake, or consult, research at all; they do not feel encouraged or enabled by their schools to do so. On the contrary, professional development for many teachers has meant merely the inculcation of new government initiatives and requirements.

No government, whether rhetorically committed to 'evidence' or not, has seriously invested in strengthening the scholarship of teaching throughout the profession, nor in ensuring that there is a creative symbiosis between professional practice and research. We do have a great and good tradition in the UK of this kind of approach and its accompanying activities, but the work is threatened because the schools and universities that have pioneered and sustained research partnerships have scarcer resources to devote and diminishing incentives to continue. In addition, schools are becoming increasingly isolated from each other, especially in terms of undertaking collaborative research projects. If the quality of the teaching profession is the key to national educational success, then truly it is time that research-informed practice was properly supported and funded by government.

Take-out messages

- **TAKE-OUT** ①: Collectively, we need to revisit the large body of research done during a decade of investment in 'evidence-based education' from 2000 to 2010, the achievements and the failures.
- **TAKE-OUT** ②: One of the lessons to be learned from those efforts is that 'finding evidence for what works' is more of a slogan than a realizable project. In teaching, what is both required and realistic is not 'evidence-based' but 'research-informed' practice.
- **TAKE-OUT** ③: Another lesson is that research-in-teaching is much more a matter of *engagement* than of *application*; the role and value of research in teaching is as a *process* of collaborative enquiry that can be modelled for students, as distinct from an epistemic *product* to be downloaded from a website.
- **TAKE-OUT** ④: Research-informed teaching requires substantial, assured, and sustained resourcing; the requisite skills and dispositions should be inculcated during initial teacher education, and reinforced and developed through ongoing professional development within learning communities.

References

Alexander, R. (2004) 'Still no pedagogy? Principle, pragmatism and compliance in primary education'. *Cambridge Journal of Education*, 34 (1), 7–33.

Bell, M., Cordingley, P., Isham, C., and Davis, R. (2010) *Report of Professional Practitioner Use of Research Review: Practitioner engagement in and/or with research*. Coventry: CUREE, GTCE, LSIS, and NTRP.

Blunkett, D. (2000) 'Influence or irrelevance: Can social science improve government?' *Research Intelligence*, 71, 12–22. Reprint of speech made at a meeting convened by the Economic and Social Research Council, 2 February.

Broadfoot, P. (1988) 'Educational research: Two cultures and three estates'. *British Educational Research Journal*, 14 (1), 3–15.

Brown, C., and Rogers, S. (2014) 'Knowledge creation as an approach to facilitating evidence-informed practice: Examining ways to measure the success of using this method with early years practitioners in Camden (London)'. *Journal of Educational Change*, 16 (1), 79–99. Early online publication. http://link.springer.com/article/10.1007/s10833-014-9238-9 (accessed 19 January 2015; requires subscription)..

Byatt, A.S. (1997) *Babel Tower*. London: Vintage.

Davies, H.T.O., Nutley, S.M., and Smith, P.C. (eds) (2000) *What Works? Evidence-Based Policy and Practice in Public Services*. Bristol: Policy Press.

Davies, P. (1999) 'What is evidence-based education?' *British Journal of Educational Studies*, 47 (2), 108–21.

Desforges, C. (2009) 'Foreword'. In Morris, A. *Evidence Matters: Towards informed professionalism for educators*. Reading: CfBT Education Trust, 3–4.

Elliott, J. (1996) 'School effectiveness research and its critics: Alternative visions of schooling'. *Cambridge Journal of Education*, 26 (2), 199–224.

— (2001) 'Making evidence-based practice educational'. *British Educational Research Journal*, 27 (5), 555–74.

Engeström, Y. (2007) 'Studying learning and development as expansive phenomena'. Paper presented at a public seminar, Oxford University Department of Educational Studies, Oxford, 15 January.

Furlong, J., and Salisbury, J. (2005) 'Best practice research scholarships: An evaluation'. *Research Papers in Education*, 20 (1), 45–83.

General Teaching Council (2008) 'Discussion 1: The importance of teacher expertise'. Online. http://cloudworks.ac.uk/cloud/view/3539 (accessed 12 September 2014).

Goldacre, B. (2013) *Building Evidence into Education*. London: Department for Education. Online. http://media.education.gov.uk/assets/files/pdf/b/ben%20goldacre%20paper.pdf (accessed 25 January 2015).

Griffiths, J. (2003) *NFER: The first fifty years 1946–1996*. Slough: National Foundation for Educational Research.

Hargreaves, D. (1996) *Teaching as a Research-Based Profession: Possibilities and prospects (Teacher Training Agency Annual Lecture 1996)*. London: Teacher Training Agency.

Haynes, L., Service, O., Goldacre, B., and Torgerson, D. (2012) *Test, Learn, Adapt: Developing public policy with randomised controlled trials*. London: Cabinet Office.

Hillage, J., Pearson, R., Anderson, A., and Tamkin, P. (1998) *Excellence in Research on Schools*. London: Department for Education and Employment.

Ioannidis, J.P.A. (2005) 'Why most published research findings are false'. *Public Library of Science Medicine*, 2 (8), e124.

Lingard, B., and Renshaw, P. (2010) 'Teaching as a research-informed and research-informing profession'. In Campbell, A., and Groundwater-Smith, S. (eds) *Connecting Inquiry and Professional Learning in Education: International perspectives and practical solutions*. Abingdon: Routledge, 26–39.

McIntyre, D. (2005) 'Bridging the gap between research and practice'. *Cambridge Journal of Education*, 35 (3), 357–82.

Petty, G. (2009) *Evidence-Based Teaching: A practical approach*. Cheltenham: Nelson Thornes.

Rickinson, M., Aspinall, C., Clark, A., Dawson, L., McLeod, S., Poulton, P., Rogers, J., and Sargent, J. (2003) *Connecting Research and Practice: Education for sustainable development*. Southwell: British Educational Research Association.

Rudduck, J., and Hopkins, D. (eds) (1985) *Research as a Basis for Teaching: Readings from the work of Lawrence Stenhouse*. London: Heinemann Educational Books.

Saunders, L. (2007) *Supporting Teachers' Engagement in and with Research*. London: Teaching and Learning Research Programme. Online. www.tlrp.org/capacity/rm/wt/saunders2.html (accessed 14 September 2014).

— (2010) 'The changing role of research in education'. *Education Today*, 60 (2), 16–21.

— (2014) '"Decoro, Sprezzatura, Grazia": A creative metaphor for teaching and teachers' learning today?' *Professional Development Today*, 16 (2), 12–20.

Thomas, G., and Pring, R. (eds) (2004) *Evidence-Based Practice in Education*. Maidenhead: Open University Press.

White, V. (2007) 'Schools research in the English Ministry of Education: An inside view'. In Saunders, L. (ed.) *Educational Research and Policy-Making: Exploring the border country between research and policy*. London: Routledge 19–34.

Chapter 4

Using evidence, learning, and the role of professional learning communities
Louise Stoll

Chapter overview

Being able to collaborate to make the best use of evidence to enhance teacher practice is fundamental to successful teaching today. In this chapter, I first describe three evidence sources: student and other data; teacher research or enquiry projects; and external research findings. Next, I consider different perspectives on the social learning that takes place when teachers engage with evidence. I argue that professional learning communities provide the ideal home for evidence-informed practice, and that they are what bring evidence to life. I offer four reasons for this. The chapter concludes with a set of suggestions for leadership of evidence-rich professional learning communities.

Using evidence, learning, and the role of professional learning communities

Around the world, teacher professionalism is seen as crucial to improving school quality. The authors of an OECD report called for significant change in teachers' practice and development, arguing that education today demands 'high-level knowledge workers who constantly advance their own professional knowledge as well as that of their profession' (Istance *et al.*, 2012: 36). Being able to make the best use of evidence to enhance teacher practice is fundamental to realizing this ideal. But that is not all: an expectation of collective responsibility underlies the quotation. This is about knowledge work for the good of colleagues – not acting as a lone ranger or becoming an individual star. The international picture is also one of increasing collaboration between teachers within and across schools. How do evidence use and teacher collaboration fit together?

Where does evidence come in?

A recognized and increasingly important feature of high-quality professionalism, especially knowledge work, involves engaging with evidence and in evidence gathering to inform practice. This means collecting, analysing, and using data and impact evidence; carrying out research, enquiry, and evaluation that produces evidence; and using externally generated research findings. These frequently can be interlinked. But while we know that using evidence and promoting its use are critical to improving practice, we also know that these things are often performed in a superficial way. There are still relatively few schools that are hotbeds of teacher enquiry, and few schools have staff libraries or promote 'the research article of the week'. What is missing?

Social learning: A key ingredient

While acknowledging meta-analyses as 'a compelling evidence base of a particular kind', Andy Hargreaves and Michael Fullan caution that although it is important to know which practices have large positive effects:

> A list like this has little value by itself unless you are working with a group of other professionals sharpening the operational meaning of the items on it, and determining how and when to use these different strategies with one's own students.
>
> (Hargreaves and Fullan, 2012: 51–2)

This takes us back to the issue of collaboration for improvement and transformation. It is a myth that intelligence is just an individual concept (Lucas and Claxton, 2010). Thinking interdependently, being able to work and learn well with other people, and learning from and with others is what Art Costa and Bena Kallick (2000) called a habit of an intelligent mind.

Most people do not need persuading that connecting is central to our lives. Social networking is now a norm for most of us. Many readers of this chapter will have 'grown up digital' (Tapscott, 2009: 2); in other words, 'digital technology is no more intimidating than a VCR or toaster'. We are becoming natural collaborators, staying in touch on mobile devices wherever we are. And as employees, Don Tapscott and colleagues' research found, Net Geners want to work hand-in-hand with colleagues to create better goods and services, design products, influence decisions, and improve work processes. But, although social-networking sites help people to connect, they do not necessarily produce collective intelligence (Leadbeater, 2008). How can people's natural desire to collaborate best be harnessed into learning power – collaborating with others, learning with and from them, to achieve personal and collective goals? Let us look more closely at social learning.

What is happening when you are learning together?

Learning with and from others is a natural way to learn. Metaphors can help us think about learning in different ways (Sfard, 1998). One metaphor is acquisition: learning is about acquiring knowledge, understanding, and skills. Social constructivism, the underpinning social learning theory, proposes that the learner, drawing on their prior knowledge and experience, makes meaning of new information or problems through talk – sharing, challenging, negotiating, and justifying ideas (Vygotsky, 1978).

Social constructivism, when applied to children's learning, often focuses on the teacher's role as guide. In adult learning, social constructivism might be applied to some forms of coaching or a mentoring conversation between a more experienced mentor and their mentee. Most people sometimes appreciate the guidance of someone more experienced, saying 'have you tried ...?' But that great suggestion may not work in everyone's context. Research on the transfer of practice found that it can be more powerful when relationships between those involved are more equal, as Michael Fielding and colleagues (2005) and Judy Sebba and colleagues (2012) describe it, through 'joint practice development'.

Participation is a second social learning metaphor, drawn from social-cultural theories of learning. The main idea is that learning occurs through participating in activity within a cultural context. In Communities of Practice (CoPs) individuals learn by engaging in contributing to the practice of their communities, and the community learns by refining its practice and ensuring there are new generations of members (Lave and Wenger, 1991). CoPs are groups of people sharing a concern, a set of problems, or a passion about a topic, who deepen their knowledge and expertise in this area by ongoing interaction. Basically, a CoP combines three elements (Wenger, 1998):

- a *domain* of knowledge, defining a set of issues and creating common ground and a sense of common identity
- a *community* of people who care about this domain and who foster interactions and relationships based on mutual respect and trust
- the shared *practice* (i.e. frameworks, ideas, tools, information, language, stories, documents, etc.) the community is developing to be effective in their domain.

An extension of this, and another way of looking at learning that has become increasingly popular as interest in innovative practice grows, is thinking of it as creation – specifically knowledge creation (Paavola *et al.*, 2004). This draws from organizational learning theory. The argument goes that talk between colleagues helps transform tacit knowledge (what we know but do not articulate) into explicit knowledge and the social process involved helps create new shared knowledge; learning as creating something new (Nonaka and Takeuchi, 1995).

Using just one of these metaphors cannot capture the richness of social learning. A more comprehensive picture may be gained by drawing on all of them. But how can social learning be put to work in the service of evidence-informed practice?

Professional learning communities: Bringing evidence to life

Social learning is, or should be, embedded in the DNA of professional learning communities. Professional learning communities are groups of people within or across schools or, in their most ideal form, whole staffs, who are driven by a common desire to make a difference for all their pupils, and who collaborate as they investigate their practices and any other valuable evidence they can lay their hands on to find the interventions that promote the best learning (Stoll and Louis, 2007). Professional learning communities are the collaborative cultures within which evidence-informed practice can be seeded and nurtured so as to flourish. It can make a real difference when schools develop professional learning communities. Where they persistently focus on improving learning and teaching, they improve teachers' practice and pupils' learning (Vescio *et al.*, 2008). Why, then, are professional learning communities such ideally suited homes for evidence-informed practice?

- *Enquiry and testing research ideas is 'the way we do things'.* Investigation and enquiry are core activities. Teachers develop expertise through analysing their interactions with students and being open to evidence of the impact they have (Hattie, 2012). They are curious and even eager to try out ideas that have been shown to be effective elsewhere, for example through the meta-analyses carried out by John Hattie for Visible Learning or included in the Sutton Trust/ Educational Endowment Foundation toolkit. But, as Hattie says, they use these as a source for forming their own professional judgements:

they are the ones creating contextually appropriate knowledge as they generate new ideas and evidence-informed practices.

- *Challenging thinking is actively encouraged.* Professional learning communities are characterized by trusting and mutually respectful relationships. Because of this, teachers are not afraid to speak directly because it might offend someone. Cultural norms are such that it is expected that colleagues will act as each other's critical friends, challenging assumptions and thinking. And powerful professional learning that makes a difference to teachers' practice and students' learning does exactly that: it challenges people's thinking (Timperley, 2011; Stoll *et al.*, 2012). As Steven Katz and Lisa Dack (2013) describe it, people's assumptions are interrupted. Evidence can be a great way to challenge thinking when it contradicts what you think you know. It can stop the 'if it ain't broke, don't fix it' mentality.

- *Learning conversations are commonplace.* Members of communities connect through dialogue: all participants play equal roles, suspending their individual assumptions as they enter into a genuine 'thinking together' (Senge, 1990). This fits well with joint practice development's emphasis on equality. People listen to each other. But in professional learning communities the learning goal is more overt, as people engage in learning conversations that challenge their thinking about how they have been tackling an issue. New evidence can provide an important stimulus for learning conversations. Teachers' tacit knowledge, including any presuppositions, ideas, and beliefs are brought to the surface, examined, challenged, and combined with their colleagues' knowledge and the external knowledge of the evidence. Collective intelligence is harnessed, and new ideas and practices are created as initial knowledge is enhanced or transformed through the conversation (Earl and Timperley, 2008). So learning conversations are the way that teachers make meaning together and jointly come up with new insights and knowledge that lead to intentional change to enhance their practice and student learning (Stoll, 2012). Exploring evidence, participants offer diverse perspectives, challenge each other in respectful ways, and are open to being honest and pushing themselves to reflect deeply in ways that challenge their thinking.

- *People think about the best ways to exchange knowledge.* Professional learning communities use evidence to create new knowledge that they will then aim to move around the school and other schools in a spirit of collective responsibility. Sharing knowledge with others can be challenging. Evidence-informed practice that works well for some teachers may not easily translate into different contexts. Yet a core activity of professional learning communities is sharing knowledge to help enhance others' practice. Knowledge needs bringing to life in ways that will help others to engage with the ideas, locate them within their context and in relation to prior experiences and learning, make meaning, and construct new knowledge from them. This involves a social process of making learning connections that I call *knowledge animation* (Stoll, 2010). The word 'animate' comes from the Latin word 'anima' which means breath, life, or soul. To animate is to bring something to life, to put it in motion. It suggests action and movement, dynamism and vibrancy, invigoration and innovation. The focus of knowledge animation is helping people to learn and use knowledge generated elsewhere and, through it, to create valuable new knowledge.

As professional learning communities generate evidence-informed knowledge they want to share, they should be thinking of knowledge animation strategies that will help others make those necessary learning connections. Professional learning communities need to ask themselves questions such as: what animation tools and processes are going to help people learn, use, or adapt and exchange particular knowledge best? In other words, what tools and processes will be most powerful in helping people to expand their repertoires and change their understanding, attitudes, and behaviours? External evidence, whether from academic research or teachers' collaborative enquiry, needs presenting in ways that will interest others, enable them to process the external ideas within the frame of their own experience, and explore implications for their own context. As already discussed, it also needs to challenge assumptions if new learning is to take place, as people reflect on how it fits with their own prior knowledge and contexts and then combine it with prior knowledge to create new knowledge, which they will then use to enhance their practice.

Leading learning in evidence-rich professional learning communities

Evidence-rich professional learning communities require intentional leadership. Proactive individuals will always exist in schools, with innovators and early adopters of new ideas (Rogers, 1971) creatively developing their practice by drawing on evidence and using evidence in different ways. But ensuring that evidence-informed practice is a school-wide or school-to-school network-wide reality depends on ensuring supportive conditions: in short, you need the right culture, structures, and learning opportunities.

My own and others' research and R&D activities have found a number of helpful ways to lead learning in evidence-rich professional learning communities (also see *resource box 4.1*):

- *Be evidence passionate.* Evidence-passionate leaders are deeply curious about finding out what will make the most positive difference to their own students' learning in the broadest sense. They understand that practice does not necessarily have all the answers and they value academic research because it can provide one important external perspective. Their own enquiry habit of mind (Earl and Katz, 2006a) leads them to look for a range of perspectives on problems, purposefully seek relevant information from diverse sources, and investigate and explore ideas until they are clearer about what they mean. Registering for their own higher degrees, participating in reading groups, collaborating on the peer reviews of each other's schools that several networks and partnerships now organize, or joining projects with local networks or universities where they carry out focused learning enquiries and data analysis with other headteachers, senior leaders, or middle leaders are just a few examples I have experienced and come across both in England and internationally. The leaders are both learning and modelling the fact that evidence matters.

- *Promote enquiry habits of mind.* As well as modelling, this means leaders taking every opportunity to create a culture throughout and across their schools where enquiry is a habit of mind that routinely challenges colleagues' assumptions and practices, and helps them make well-evidenced decisions that are more likely to lead to success. If teachers are going to become more open to learning, to experimenting with new evidence-informed practices, and collaborating with colleagues to evaluate their success, they have to feel safe to do so. Developing trust – relationships first (Kaser and Halbert, 2009) – is vital, both in relationships between teachers and leaders, and in relationships between teachers. A teacher will not open up their practice to a colleague's 'scrutiny' (i.e. observation) if it feels risky to do so. Creating a culture in which staff are open to taking the kind of risk involved in doing something different is fundamental to introducing new practice (Stoll and Temperley, 2009).

- *Facilitate deep exchange, including providing time and space.* If teachers are going to engage in serious and evidence-informed analysis of their practice, and in deep learning conversations, the context needs to be carefully planned to facilitate this. There is no getting away from it; powerful professional learning – and, indeed, any other learning – requires time (Stoll *et al.*, 2003). Whether covering classes themselves, finding ways to rearrange timetables, having colleagues or recently retired teachers covering classes, or finding other ways to free staff up, it is absolutely essential that teachers have the necessary time to engage in evidence-informed collaborative practice development. Some of this might be arranged outside of school time, but where observation and some other activities are concerned, it has to take place during the school day. Creative use of technology is now enabling teachers to observe classrooms elsewhere in their own and other schools, and social media can support teacher engagement with evidence, as long as attention is paid to ensuring that the technology facilitates meaningful exchange. Development of coaching and facilitation skills among staff members also helps to support learning conversations and the development of internal critical friendship.

- *Make connections with research partners and other critical friends.* Over many years, research has frequently been viewed as the domain of academics in ivory towers. While researchers have their own imperatives and motivations, many passionately believe that their own and others' research has much to offer teachers and leaders that can help them enhance practice. In addition to their external theories and findings, which need animating, they can offer schools rigour, and research and evaluation skills. Collaborations between practitioners and researchers potentially can make a real difference to students' learning experiences and outcomes. There are many excellent examples, but it may require changes in some school–university relationships to develop more powerful partnerships. Teachers and leaders need critical friends who will ask challenging questions. Academics can ask these, as can colleagues in other schools who can also become partners in collaborative enquiry and peer review, providing a much wider landscape for colleagues to gather evidence and investigate practice.

- *Have a theory of action.* Leaders need to think seriously about why and how the teaching and learning practices they decide to support in their school will make a positive difference to students. They also need to articulate this and check whether their hypotheses are correct. If the practices need adjustment, or even changing entirely, they need to take action to do this and continue to monitor the situation with mini feedback loops, constantly moving practice forward so that it has the greatest chance of being successful. Chris Argyris and Donald Schön

(1974) describe how people have two theories of action. The first is an explicit 'espoused' theory of action that they explain to others about why they behave in a certain way. But their 'theory-in-use' is the unspoken theory that actually governs what they do. Successful practice depends on the two theories being congruent with each other. Creating a theory of action or theory of change requires identifying a desirable end goal – or, as Lorna Earl and Steven Katz (2006b) describe it, 'starting with the end in mind' (i.e. the student learning you are seeking). You then work backwards through intermediate outcomes, establishing links between these and the goal, listing causes and effects, then working out which activities are leading to which outcomes, and identifying what else is needed for your interventions to work. Starting with the end in mind about a student learning issue means encouraging and supporting teachers in gathering the evidence from students, parents, and each other up front to deepen their understanding of the issue. External research reviews may help provide evidence about what worked in other contexts, but this does not guarantee it will work in your own situation. That is why it is important to think about your theory of action and be ready to refine it as necessary.

- *Work towards sustainability.* Finally, leaders think about change that lasts. I find Andy Hargreaves and Dean Fink's (2000) framing of three elements of system reform helpful here. A school is a system, and so is a group of schools. What leaders are aiming for is sustainability: this is what the DNA part is about. Hargreaves and Fink write about the importance of depth, breadth, and length. Depth, in relation to evidence use, is thoughtful, professional, informed practice that is underpinned by a deep understanding of what leads to the best learning experiences and outcomes for individuals and whole groups of students, and an ability to articulate why and how this makes a difference. Breadth means that it is not just mavericks or 'keenies' who are thinking about and using evidence. Evidence use has gone viral. And length means that using evidence really is just 'part of the way we do things'.

RESOURCE BOX **4.1:**
Stoll, L., Bolam, R., MacMahon, A., Thomas, S., Wallace, M., Greenwood, A., and Hawkey, K. (2006) *Professional Learning Communities: Source materials for school leaders and other leaders of professional learning.* London: Innovation Unit, NCSL and GTC.

These materials, based on the results of the first national study of professional learning communities (PLCs) in England (Bolam *et al.*, 2005), were designed as knowledge animation tools to help: (1) promote understanding of and engagement with the idea and practice of PLCs with particular reference to people's own contexts; and (2) to stimulate PLCs by promoting self-evaluation, reflective enquiry, dialogue, collaborative learning, and problem solving. They are available at: www.lcll.org.uk/professional-learning-communities.html.

Collaborating with others is a means of ensuring that young learners across our schools have equally high-quality opportunities. By developing professional learning communities with peers, locally, nationally, and internationally, teachers and school leaders can share and tease out principles of good practice, engage in deep and challenging conversations, create knowledge to respond to particular issues that any one person might find it hard to resolve, observe colleagues elsewhere, experience fresh perspectives, reduce narrow and isolated thinking, and see their own school through a different lens.

Take-out messages

In the spirit of this chapter's topic, these take-out messages are posed as questions to feed into learning conversations:

- **TAKE-OUT ①:** To be successful, teachers today need to collaborate to generate and make the best use of evidence to enhance their practice. How well do evidence use and teacher collaboration fit together in your context? What are the challenges in connecting them and how might these be resolved?
- **TAKE-OUT ②:** Learning together is a natural process. What kinds of social learning can be found in your school/across your schools? What sorts of metaphors would you use to describe this learning and why?
- **TAKE-OUT ③:** If professional learning communities are the collaborative cultures within which evidence-informed practice can be seeded and nurtured so as to flourish, in what ways is your community's culture strongly collaborative and what are the priorities for development?
- **TAKE-OUT ④:** To share and exchange evidence-informed knowledge with others, it needs animating – bringing to life. What are the most successful strategies you have designed or come across to animate knowledge?

- **TAKE-OUT** ⑤: Having a theory of action about practice helps you to articulate the results you expect from your practice and the reasons for them. What is your theory of action around using evidence in your school/across your schools and how will you test it?

References

Argyris, C., and Schön, D.A. (1974) *Theory in Practice: Increasing professional effectiveness*. San Francisco, CA: Jossey-Bass.

Bolam, R., McMahon, A., Stoll, L., Thomas, S., Wallace, M., Greenwood, A., Hawkey, K., Ingram, M., Atkinson, A., and Smith, M. (2005) *Creating and Sustaining Effective Professional Learning Communities* (Research Report 637). London: Department for Education and Skills and University of Bristol.

Costa, A., and Kallick, B. (2000) *Activating and Engaging Habits of Mind*. Alexandria, VA: Association of Supervision and Curriculum Development.

Earl, L., and Katz, S. (2006a) *Leading Schools in a Data-Rich World: Harnessing data for school improvement*. Thousand Oaks, CA: Corwin.

— (2006b) *How Networked Learning Communities Work* (Seminar Series Paper 155). Melbourne: Centre for Strategic Education.

Earl, L., and Timperley, H. (2008) *Professional Learning Conversations: Challenges in using evidence for improvement*. Dordrecht: Springer.

Fielding, M., Bragg, S., Craig, J., Cunningham, I., Eraut, M., Gillinson, S., Horne, M., Robinson, C., and Thorp, J. (2005) *Factors Influencing the Transfer of Good Practice* (DfES Research Report RR 615). Nottingham: Department for Education and Skills and University of Sussex.

Hargreaves, A., and Fink, D. (2000) 'The three dimensions of reform'. *Educational Leadership*, 57 (7), 30–4.

Hargreaves, A., and Fullan, M. (2012) *Professional Capital: Transforming teaching in every school*. New York: Teachers College Press.

Hattie, J. (2012) *Visible Learning for Teachers: Maximizing impact on learning*. London: Routledge.

Istance, D., and Vincent-Lancrin, S., with Van Damme, D., Schleicher, A., and Weatherby, K. (2012) 'Preparing teachers to deliver 21st-century skills'. In Schleicher, A. (ed.) *Preparing Teachers and Developing School Leaders for the 21st Century: Lessons from around the world*. Paris: OECD, 33–54.

Kaser, L., and Halbert, J. (2009) *Leadership Mindsets: Innovation and learning in the transformation of schools*. London: Routedge.

Katz, S., and Dack, L.A. (2013) *Intentional Interruption: Breaking down learning barriers to transform professional practice*. Thousand Oaks, CA: Corwin Press.

Lave, J., and Wenger, E. (1991) *Situated Learning: Legitimate peripheral participation*. New York: Cambridge University Press.

Leadbeater, C. (2008) *We-Think: Mass innovation, not mass production*. London: Profile.

Lucas, B., and Claxton, G. (2010) *New Kinds of Smart: How the science of learnable intelligence is changing education*. Maidenhead: Open University Press.

Nonaka, I., and Takeuchi, H. (1995) *The Knowledge-Creating Company: How Japanese companies create the dynamics of innovation*. New York: Oxford University Press.

Paavola, S., Lipponen, L., and Hakkarainen, K. (2004) 'Models of innovative knowledge communities and three metaphors of learning'. *Review of Educational Research*, 74 (4), 557–76.

Rogers, E.M. (1971) *Diffusion of Innovations*. New York: Free Press.

Sebba, J., Kent, P., and Tregenza, J. (2012) *Joint Practice Development (JPD): What does the evidence suggest are effective approaches?* Nottingham: National College for School Leadership and University of Sussex.

Senge, P. (1990) *The Fifth Discipline: The art and practice of the learning organization*. New York: Doubleday.

Sfard, A. (1998) 'On two metaphors for learning and the dangers of choosing just one'. *Educational Researcher*, 27 (2), 4–13.

Stoll, L. (2010) 'Connecting learning communities: Capacity building for systemic change'. In Hargreaves, A., Lieberman, A., Fullan, M., and Hopkins, D. (eds) *Second International Handbook of Educational Change*. Dordrecht: Springer, 469–84.

— (2012) 'Stimulating learning conversations'. *Professional Development Today*, 15 (1), 6–12.

Stoll, L., Fink, D., and Earl, L. (2003) *It's About Learning (and It's About Time): What's in it for schools?* London: RoutledgeFalmer.

Stoll, L., Harris, A., and Handscomb, G. (2012) *Great Professional Development Which Leads to Great Pedagogy: Nine claims from research*. Nottingham: National College for School Leadership.

Stoll, L., and Louis, K.S. (2007) *Professional Learning Communities: Divergence, depth and dilemmas*. Maidenhead: Open University Press/McGraw Hill.

Stoll, L., and Temperley, J. (2009) 'Creative leadership: A challenge of our times'. *School Leadership and Management*, 29 (1), 65–78.

Tapscott, D. (2009) *Grown Up Digital: How the net generation is changing your world*. London: McGraw-Hill.

Timperley, H. (2011) *Realizing the Power of Professional Learning*. Maidenhead: Open University Press.

Vescio, V., Ross, D., and Adams, A. (2008) 'A review of research on the impact of professional learning communities on teaching practice and student learning'. *Teaching and Teacher Education*, 24 (1), 80–91.

Vygotsky, L.S. (1978) *Mind in Society: The development of the higher psychological processes*. Cambridge, MA: Harvard University Press.

Wenger, E. (1998) *Communities of Practice: Learning, meaning and identity*. New York: Cambridge University Press.

Chapter 5

Middle leaders as catalysts for evidence-informed change

Louise Stoll and Chris Brown

Chapter overview

Middle leaders are well placed to spread best practice both within and across schools and alliances. In this chapter we build on the findings of an Economic and Social Research Council-funded project undertaken in partnership with Challenge Partners to argue that middle leaders can often be the most effective drivers of evidence-informed change and should be harnessed to do this. First, we describe the background to the project and the partnership. Next we outline the project's aims and design, including the selection of middle leader 'catalyst' participants. Finally, we offer seven 'learnings' from the project that we are taking forward into other R&D activity and that we hope will be of value to readers.

The role of middle leaders

Over recent years, there has been greater awareness in England of the important role middle leaders can play in school improvement. Middle leaders – known in some other countries as teacher leaders – are the key link between teachers and a school's senior leaders. As such, they are well positioned to offer support and challenge to teachers and lead their learning both within their own school and across partner schools. How successful they are at this, in an evidence-hungry policy environment, will depend at least partly on their capacity to exchange high-quality research and practice knowledge and track its impact on changes in practice and improvement in pupils' learning opportunities and outcomes. In short, middle leaders have the potential to be catalysts for evidence-informed change.

We had the opportunity to explore this issue in a year-long R&D project, funded through the Economic and Social Research Council's (ESRC) Knowledge Exchange Opportunities Scheme, which we carried out in partnership with Challenge Partners. Challenge Partners (CP) is a charity owned and led by a partnership of more than 250 schools across England. CP's website states:

> We ... recognise that we are stronger together and that collaboration is the key to continued success. We exist to support schools in that role by facilitating constructive collaboration and challenge between them and providing a platform for activities which would not be possible for a school to undertake on its own. Together we aspire to become a world class, knowledge sharing community, which leads the way in school improvement and raises the standards of education for all.
>
> (http://challengepartners.org/aboutus)

What we did

In partnership with Challenge Partners we decided on the specific project focuses, recruited participants, designed and carried out project activities, and organized a parallel evaluation.

Focusing our project

Challenge Partners was concerned that many of its middle leaders did not know the most effective ways to share or exchange research or practice-based knowledge with middle leader peers and teachers in their own and other schools. They are also frequently unsure as to how best to track the impact of their professional learning and interventions on their own and teachers' practice. CP wants to embed a culture of shared outstanding research-informed practice across its partnership that is oriented towards making an impact on teaching and pupil outcomes. The group has more than twenty local hubs, each with between 4 and 21 schools. CP was keen to test out and establish such knowledge exchange among middle leaders located in different schools, who would then extend this to their hubs and beyond.

The ESRC was looking for projects that both promoted the impact of social science research and fitted with one of its own strategic aims. With our own commitment to understanding and supporting change, we were attracted to the ESRC's focus on influencing behaviour and informing interventions. Our project design was intended to help Challenge Partners' middle leaders' network start on this journey, while providing better understanding of the ways in which middle leaders' behaviours change and stimulate change among the middle leaders and their teacher colleagues. These four project questions were decided jointly:

1. What do we know about effective middle leadership within and across schools that changes teachers' practice?

2. What are powerful ways to share knowledge about excellent middle leadership practice within and across schools?
3. What evidence-based tools can be designed collaboratively between Challenge Partners' middle leaders and academic partners to track changes in teachers' practice as a result of middle leaders' interventions?
4. What leadership conditions in schools help develop and embed cultures of shared outstanding practice?

Finding change agents

Middle leaders who were, or who showed potential to be, change agents were our target group. We chose the name 'catalyst' to describe project participants in the hope that they would precipitate and stimulate big change. Although the definition of a chemical catalyst states that a catalyst (substance) is chemically unchanged by the chemical reaction or process it causes, in line with understandings about effective professional learning (Stoll *et al.*, 2012) and its impact (Guskey, 2000; Earley and Porritt, 2014), the intention was to challenge catalysts' thinking with research evidence, supporting them in designing new tools and practices to trial, refine, and evaluate.

CP started its search for catalysts in its existing subject networks. They asked hub leaders and headteachers to suggest middle leaders who were confident in their own practice, influential with peers, effective at working with colleagues in their own and other schools, interested in working with us to answer the project questions, and wanted to keep developing practice and knowledge through working in school-to-school networks. Potential catalysts were told that the aim was to collaborate with them, supporting them to:

- discover and then share knowledge across their schools about excellent middle leadership practice that has an impact
- develop effective ways to share this knowledge with their Challenge Partner hub colleagues, and middle leaders beyond their immediate network, to benefit a broader range of educators
- co-develop evidence-based tools to track ways in which they changed and enhanced their own and teachers' practice as a result of this knowledge exchange
- find ways to promote sustainable norms of between-school knowledge exchange.

Sixteen middle leaders participated in baseline telephone interviews, although last minute attendees meant that 24 participants came to the first workshop, some for a one-off experience. Fifteen middle leaders completed the project.

Designing and carrying out project activities

Project activities involved:

- four workshops where research findings and best practice were shared and blended in innovative ways and the catalysts used new learning to create and refine processes and tools to help them lead more effectively and track their impact
- face-to-face and social networking activities between workshops where the catalysts tested new ideas and trialled tools in their own and other schools
- catalysts evaluating the experiences and the impact on themselves and colleagues
- jointly developing processes to embed the notion of sharing high-quality research-informed practice between schools in their own networks and for practitioners in other networks.

In a parallel evaluation, CP practitioner research partners collaborated with us in collecting information about middle leaders' starting knowledge, beliefs, and skills and their schools' orientation to sharing outstanding practice with others. Evaluators followed project activities, observing what happened, and talking with participants about their experiences. Findings were shared with participants throughout, and fed into process improvements.

A particularly important feature for us was the combining of research and practitioner knowledge. For example, in the first workshop we fed back catalysts' baseline perceptions about effective middle leadership, which they processed in groups, generating overarching concepts. We then fed in research findings on effective middle leadership, taking them through the same process, before facilitating them in combining the knowledge into a list of 'golden nuggets' – a name suggested by a CP headteacher who was one of our informal advisers. In every subsequent workshop, we refined or added to the nuggets as further experience and/or research enriched our understanding. These were pulled together in the last workshop, where we also discussed ways in which they could most effectively be shared with other middle leaders. A similar combination process was used to support catalysts' understanding of how to track and evidence change by designing impact tools.

What we have learnt

Our experience provided rich learning about evidence-informed change that we summarize in seven points.

1) Evidence-informed change can be powerful in partnership

In Challenge Partners' desire to facilitate constructive collaboration and challenge and develop a knowledge-sharing community, they connect with a range of partners, the UCL Institute of Education being a key one. Partnership is also a key feature of the UCL Institute of Education's mission. But universities and schools, or networks of schools, often have different goals. Like any partnership or professional learning community (Stoll *et al.*, 2006), which is what we aimed to be, we needed to come to a shared agreement about the project aims and activities. The amount of time required for this should not be underestimated. In many project meetings, emails, and phone calls involving CP staff, supporting headteachers, and senior leaders, we shared workshop drafts, research instruments, and plans. A catalyst helped us to plan and present a workshop, and others were also invited to do this. Another middle leader led a session on technology use for knowledge exchange.

In an early workshop, we asked the catalysts, working in groups, to describe in simple statements what genuine knowledge exchange between practitioners and researchers meant to them. Responses were illuminating. It was clear that they thought such exchange should be focused on having an impact on their pupils and them, as these statements affirm: 'Has student learning at the heart'; 'Must have an impact on learning'; 'Will develop middle leaders and reflect on their practice'; and 'Will support developing middle leaders'.

One group then focused on implications for researchers: 'Has the potential for huge impact when [research] findings are "delivered" [facilitated] in a way [face-to-face, task based] that allows for instant engagement'; and 'Needs to be practical and set in [adapted to/relevant] context – case studies, implications for practice'. In contrast, another group viewed genuine knowledge exchange between practitioners and researchers as:

> … most effective when approached as an active and collaborative process; which can be successfully translated into practical approaches within the classroom and wider learning community.

A third group took this further in viewing it as 'a symbiotic relationship that leads to progressive thinking', while some of their peers highlighted the importance of joint commitment to a relationship-building process: 'requires trust, empowerment, engagement and time so that *deep* dialogue can take place', elaborating this with the comment 'depth before breadth and bringing it alive'.

Early analysis suggests that by the end of the project most of the catalysts had a more collaborative understanding of knowledge exchange. Researchers can be partners and can also engage in genuine knowledge exchange. As one explained in a final interview:

> I felt you weren't 'telling us' what the research said but that we were exploring it and making meaning together and that was more valuable than being directed.

Although they are not co-authoring this chapter, we have arranged to write articles with catalysts. CP is also working with us and some catalysts to develop and extend the project to involve other CP middle leaders.

2) *Effective research use stems from a process that is both engaging and challenging*

Catalysts' comments about genuine knowledge exchange shine a light on the ways they believe research findings can be brought to life. We see this social process, which we call knowledge animation (Stoll, 2010), as a way that people make learning connections when engaging with research findings. Knowledge animation helps people to learn and use ideas generated elsewhere. It focuses on finding ways of making knowledge accessible in order to stimulate conversation that challenges people's thinking, promotes new understanding, and helps them generate their own evidence-informed and contextually relevant knowledge that will enhance their practice.

Engagement with research is a process of learning (Stoll, 2010; Brown and Rogers, 2014). The external expertise brought by researchers is important but insufficient for professional learning. People's tacit knowledge needs to be surfaced and blended with explicit external knowledge (Nonaka and Takeuchi, 1995) – the research knowledge. Their assumptions can then be explored and challenged in ensuing learning conversations (Earl and Timperley, 2008; Stoll, 2012) that lead to the knowledge being jointly interpreted and converted into new knowledge that can be used to change practice.

Animating knowledge is intended to help practitioners encounter research in manageable units of meaning and in accessible, varied formats. This requires protocols, tools, and processes that present evidence in ways that stimulate exploration of topics and issues, deepen engagement, aid reflection, help people articulate tacit knowledge and beliefs, aid social processing and feed conversations, and stimulate collaborative learning and enquiry.

We designed specific processes and tools to help practitioners self-evaluate and audit their situations and contexts, identify problems and think about ways to resolve them, prioritize alternatives and compare approaches, plan and take action, and lead and manage change. With the catalysts, we also designed tools to track and evaluate progress and change. One catalyst commented on how he found this structured approach to understanding and measuring impact vital. He explained how it had helped him with other initiatives that were taking place in his school; for example, on a separate lesson-study project, his was the only group to have thought about their current reality, articulating and operationalizing their vision (including using scales, tools, and metrics) and so being able to measure how far along the journey they had reached. Another catalyst's group had been struck by the power of the message 'start with the end in mind' (Earl and Katz, 2006), as used in one enquiry model (Halbert and Kaser, 2013). They had built it into their impact tool. When the catalyst trialled the tool with a middle leader colleague, she said that 'the ML was keen to jump in but I kept saying "what are we looking for?" and "we need to keep focused"'.

3) Choose potential catalysts carefully

Despite best intentions, the project 'reached' some catalysts more powerfully than others. There could be several reasons for this. The identification process, originally aimed at potential change agents, was soon opened up to any participants in middle-leader networks. When interviewed, a few headteachers indicated that they regretted suggesting or being encouraged to recommend a particular staff member. In a couple of cases, more senior leaders had ended up as participants and felt that it was not necessarily appropriate for them, even though their self-evaluations showed personal perceptions of growth. A third reason was that, despite the fact that a specific request had been made for people interested in working with researchers, a few participants only appeared keen to engage in aspects of the project where they could share experiences with other middle leaders.

Caveats aside, a large number of highly committed and energetic catalysts enthusiastically participated in workshops and tackled the challenging intersessional tasks, often very creatively. This included bringing together colleagues in their hub schools to exchange key ideas developed during the project. Some of their headteachers were clear that the catalyst representing their school was exactly the kind of excellent and influential colleague (Daly, 2010) that helps spread and embed high-quality practice. These headteachers also thought that the project had added value for their catalyst by deepening the research underpinnings and providing networking opportunities.

4) Educational change theories can help middle leaders as catalysts

If you ask leaders which academic's ideas have influenced them most over the years, many answer Michael Fullan's. Interestingly, his core focus is on educational change. Of his many books – he is a prolific writer – *The New Meaning of Educational Change* (2007) is acknowledged to be the encyclopaedia that anyone seriously studying change should read. Other books are addressed to readers who are practitioners and policymakers (he understands knowledge animation). In *Leading in a Culture of Change*, he argued that we need 'to understand change in order to lead it better' (Fullan, 2001: 34). Over the years, a number of governments internationally have taken this on board, including change in their leadership curricula. For example, leading improvement, innovation, and change is one of the Australian Institute for Teaching and School Leadership's key professional practices for school principals, and change is one of five competence areas for Norwegian school *rektors* (headteachers). In England, the National College for Teaching and School Leadership includes leading change for improvement as an elective study module within its professional qualifications and professional development for middle and senior leaders and the National Professional Qualification for Headship.

Our project showed that understanding and applying theories of change was fundamental. The participants found these research findings among the most compelling, and told us that research on change helped them to make sense of their leadership and to approach colleagues differently. We also found that their comments about other aspects of the project were frequently couched in reference to the change literature. We argue that change theory and its implications for practice should be core features of any leadership development experiences.

5) Commitment of headteachers and other line managers is essential

In this project, the catalysts were the core change agents, but they did not work in isolation. Support and backing from headteachers and other closely connected senior leaders was vital. Our findings show that catalysts need the right conditions for their interventions to work, both within and across schools. There is an analogy with chemical reactions involving other kinds of catalysts: the reaction will not occur in every situation and context (Godfrey, 2014).

As research clearly demonstrates, the effect of leadership on pupil outcomes is second only to that of teachers (Leithwood *et al.*, 2008). In addition, leaders exert their main effect by promoting and participating in teacher development (Robinson, 2011). They also create a professional learning community culture that encourages collective responsibility for, and reflective dialogue about, pupil learning and the purposeful sharing of practice (Leithwood and Louis, 2012). Catalyst interviews indicated that some headteachers and line managers were more actively interested and encouraging than others. Headteachers are extremely busy and have many staff to think about, but some schools seemed more geared up to support and make use of ideas and tools generated in project workshops and through intersessional tasks. Interviews with some headteachers suggested that while they saw the potential of impact tracking tools for middle leaders' work with colleagues in other schools, they had not considered that these tools might be useful in their own schools, beyond the specific case study teachers that catalysts had worked with. Given that using impact tools was new to every participant, we might assume that they are not commonly discussed among middle leaders in their schools. We suggest that leading evidence-informed practice involves being able to track the impact your leadership has on others' practice and being able to share that with other leaders. Headteachers are fundamentally important in creating the conditions for sharing but, to do this, they need to understand the potential of evidence-informed practice for their own school, as well as for other schools.

6) Evidence-informed change beyond their school can be challenging for middle leaders

A key goal of the project was to develop or deepen middle leader networking and catalysts' ability to work with colleagues in other schools. In a self-improving school system, as England's white paper describes it (Department for Education, 2010), it is considered essential for leaders to help colleagues in other schools. Some catalysts found this easier than others. In our final workshop, we gave everyone different coloured dots to represent who they had 'reached' during the project, also asking them to estimate the depth of colleagues' engagement. Results showed considerable disparities between catalysts in their reach beyond the school. One middle leader, for example, had made plans by the end of the project for a coaching session with a middle leader in another school, and had only had basic conversations with her headteacher. Another had only had email exchanges with hub colleagues. In contrast, another catalyst had involved eight middle leaders in an early network survey completion task, had worked with a group of teachers in another school for his case study over time, focusing on resilience, had trialled his impact tool with a group of teachers in other schools, and was using project ideas to further his work on resilience with other middle school leaders. And he was not the only one. Responses to a questionnaire asking catalysts what change agent skills they had used with different colleagues suggested that trust building was particularly important when working with colleagues in other schools.

7) *The potential of technology for spreading evidence-informed middle leadership practice is not yet realized*

Challenge Partners schools are spread around the country. There can be large distances between schools within a hub. Travelling between schools can be a challenge even if it leads to productive outcomes, as one participant told us after travelling to plan a hub exchange meeting with another catalyst: 'Because when I went over there I had such an in-depth conversation with [other catalyst's name], I felt it was worth doing'.

We spent some time in sessions exploring effective ways to share evidence, and encouraging the use of technology. Some of the catalysts were more confident social media users than the research team and the CP partners. We therefore invited a catalyst to lead a session in which he introduced several social media options, after which the catalysts chose one or another way of animating their own knowledge for middle leaders. Several catalysts also used technology to create presentations of their intersessional task findings. Studies suggest that social networking is becoming increasingly relevant in assisting teachers to reflect upon their own practice and challenge thinking (McCulloch *et al.*, 2011), and that it can facilitate evaluation activity. Our conclusion is that social media can be helpful tools to spread evidence-informed messages, although further work needs to be done in this area.

Take-out messages

- **TAKE-OUT ①**: Engagement with evidence means precisely that: practitioners are unlikely to gain any benefit from the 'dissemination' of evidence from 'experts', but they will gain if the process of engagement encourages interactive collaboration that leads to reflection and challenge.
- **TAKE-OUT ②**: The choice of 'research champions' is key: not only were the most effective catalysts keen to promote the use of evidence,

they were also influential within and beyond their schools. This meant that their peers were willing to learn from and engage with them.

- **TAKE-OUT** ③: The world is a complex place and to understand it often involves embracing that complexity. Engaging with educational theory helped our catalysts both to reconsider their practice and to find new frameworks through which to explain effective practice to others.
- **TAKE-OUT** ④: Support for research champions is vital for them to succeed. Senior leaders must provide both the structures and the cultures to facilitate evidence use. Research engagement must be established as a norm, but without providing time, space, and other resources, the interactive and collaborative elements of meaningful engagement are likely to be absent.

This work was supported by the Economic and Social Research Council [grant number: ES/L002043/1].

References

Brown, C., and Rogers, S. (2014) 'Knowledge creation as an approach to facilitating evidence-informed practice: Examining ways to measure the success of using this method with early years practitioners in Camden (London)'. *Journal of Educational Change*, 16 (1), 79–99. Early online publication. http://link.springer.com/article/10.1007/s10833-014-9238-9 (accessed 19 January 2015; requires subscription).

Daly, A. (2010) 'Mapping the terrain: Social network theory and educational change'. In Daly, A. (ed.) *Social Network Theory and Educational Change*. Cambridge, MA: Harvard Education Press, 1–16.

Department for Education (2010) *The Importance of Teaching: The schools white paper 2010*. London: The Stationery Office. Online. www.education.gov.uk/schools/toolsandinitiatives/schoolswhitepaper/b0068570/the-importance-of-teaching (accessed 30 January 2013).

Earl, L., and Katz, S. (2006) *Leading Schools in a Data-Rich World: Harnessing data for school improvement*. Thousand Oaks, CA: Corwin.

Earl, L., and Timperley, H. (2008) 'Understanding how evidence and learning conversations work'. In Earl, L., and Timperley, H. (eds) *Professional Learning Conversations: Challenges in using evidence for improvement*. Dordrecht: Springer, 1–12.

Earley, P., and Porritt, V. (2014) 'Evaluating the impact of professional development: The need for a student-focused approach'. *Professional Development in Education*, 40 (1), 112–29.

Fullan, M. (2007) *The New Meaning of Educational Change*. 4th ed. New York: Teachers College Press.

— (2001) *Leading in a Culture of Change*. San Francisco, CA: Jossey-Bass.

Godfrey, D. (2014) 'Leadership of schools as research-led organisations in the English educational environment: Cultivating a research-engaged school culture'. *Educational Management Administration & Leadership*. Early online publication. http://ema.sagepub.com/content/early/2014/02/20/1741143213508294.full (accessed 19 January 2015; requires subscription).

Guskey, T.R. (2000) *Evaluating Professional Development*. Thousand Oaks, CA: Corwin.

Halbert, J., and Kaser, L. (2013) *Spirals of Inquiry for Equity and Quality*. Vancouver: British Columbia Principals' and Vice Principals' Association.

Istance, D., and Vincent-Lancrin, S., with Van Damme, D., Schleicher, A., and Weatherby, K. (2012) 'Preparing teachers to deliver 21st-century skills'. In Schleicher, A. (ed.) *Preparing Teachers and Developing School Leaders for the 21st Century: Lessons from around the world*. Paris: OECD, 33–54.

Leithwood, K., Harris, A., and Hopkins, D. (2008) 'Seven strong claims about successful school leadership'. *School Leadership and Management*, 28 (1), 27–42.

Leithwood, K., and Louis, K.S. (2012) *Linking Leadership to Student Learning*. San Francisco, CA: Jossey-Bass.

McCulloch, J., McIntosh, E., and Barrett, T. (2011) 'Tweeting for teachers: How can social media support teacher professional development?' Online. www.itslifejimbutnotasweknowit.org.uk/files/libraryfrom2012/Tweeting-for-teachers.pdf (accessed 29 January 2012).

Nonaka, I., and Takeuchi, H. (1995) *The Knowledge-Creating Company: How Japanese companies create the dynamics of innovation*. New York: Oxford University Press.

Robinson, V. (2011) *Student-Centred Leadership*. San Francisco, CA: Jossey-Bass.

Stoll, L. (2010) 'Connecting learning communities: Capacity building for systemic change'. In Hargreaves, A., Lieberman, A., Fullan, M., and Hopkins, D. (eds) *Second International Handbook of Educational Change*. Dordrecht: Springer, 469–84.

— (2012) 'Stimulating learning conversations'. *Professional Development Today*, 14 (4), 6–12.

Stoll, L., Bolam, R., McMahon, A., Wallace, M., and Thomas, S. (2006) 'Professional learning communities: A review of the literature'. *Journal of Educational Change*, 7 (4), 221–58.

Stoll, L., Harris, A., and Handscomb, G. (2012) *Great Professional Development Which Leads to Consistently Great Pedagogy: Nine claims from research*. Online. www.gov.uk/government/publications/great-professional-development-which-leads-to-great-pedagogy-nine-claims-from-research (accessed 16 October 2014).

Chapter 6

Knowledge creation as an approach to delivering evidence-informed practice among early years practitioners in Camden (London)

Chris Brown and Sue Rogers

Chapter overview

If practitioners are to engage effectively with evidence, they will need to *combine* their understanding of school context and existing effective practice with any new perspectives such evidence provides. In accordance with this, this chapter has two key aims: first it examines our attempts to use *knowledge creation* as a way of developing this type of combined evidence-informed practice among a learning community of 36 early years practitioners in the London Borough of Camden. Second, situating the idea of effective evidence use within the notion of *expertise*, it seeks to illustrate ways of measuring evidence use. Specifically, it looks at how we sought to ascertain whether early years practitioners, having been continually engaged in knowledge-creation activity, were developing expertise as evidence users. We conclude by assessing our approach, examining both its strengths and limitations.

Evidence-informed practice

We suggest that, while the use of evidence by practitioners is 'a good thing', in itself being 'evidence-informed' seems a somewhat nebulous notion. It is difficult, for instance, to conceptualize what a 'state' of evidence-informed practice might 'look like': should we expect evidence to inform practice in a 'pure' form? In other words, do we believe that acts of practice should follow exactly what was intended by the researcher? This seems unlikely and also undesirable. Instead it seems more effective and equitable that evidence should join together with contextual and other practice-related factors and that any practice-related decisions become a function of all of these. This is reflected by England's Department for Education (DfE), who define evidence-informed practice in the following way:

> Evidence based practice is a *combination* of practitioner expertise and knowledge of the best external research, and evaluation based evidence.
>
> (Cited in Department for Children, Schools and Families, 2010: 19, authors' emphasis)

The DfE's notion of what it is to be evidence-informed, however, highlights three key issues. The first is the need to conceive of how such combinations of external research and practitioner-held knowledge might be meaningfully achieved (i.e. what represents a successful combination of these knowledge types?). The second issue is identifying approaches that will enable us to successfully combine external research and practitioner-held knowledge, so that a state of being 'evidence-informed' is achieved. Last, there is the need to measure whether we have reached our destination: how might we ascertain whether practitioners are now informed by evidence? We use this chapter to discuss these issues in relation to the Camden Early Years Learning Community project.

Expertise

One possible way to conceptualize the combination of evidence types described above, is to consider Flyvbjerg's notions of 'expertise' in relation to evidence use (e.g. see Brown, 2013, 2014). Flyvbjerg (2001) employs the 'Dreyfus' model of learning to illustrate what he means by expertise, an approach that employs five 'levels' of human learning, ranging from 'novice' to 'expert'.[1] What the Dreyfus model clarifies is that each of these five levels comprises recognizably different behaviours in relation to the performance of a given skill. A novice, for example, will be new to a particular situation, and will, during instruction, learn about *facts* corresponding to, and other characteristics pertaining to, the situation and so is taught or develops 'rules for action'. As learners advance from 'novice' through the levels of 'advanced beginner', 'competent performer', and 'proficient performer', however, a number of things occur.

First, instances of performing in real-life situations increase, and as a result the number of 'cases' that the learner encounters and tackles also increases. Second, recognition of different situations accumulates, as does recognition of the context in which those situations occur. Third, dependency on specific 'rules for action' diminishes as learners are able to interpret and judge how to perform optimally in any given situation. Genuine expertise, though, only occurs as the result of a 'quantum leap' in behaviour and perception. Specifically, expertise results as an individual moves from being an analytical problem solver to someone who: '[exhibits] thinking and behaviour that is rapid, intuitive, holistic, interpretive ... [expertise] has no immediate similarity to the slow, analytical reasoning which characterises rational problem-solving and the first three levels of the learning process' (Flyvbjerg, 2001: 14). In other words, true expertise represents a situation in which experience and external evidence are intuitively and holistically combined in order that a problem might be immediately assessed and a solution provided almost without conscious reasoning.

Professional learning communities

We now consider approaches that enable external and practitioner evidence to be combined in ways consistent with Flyvbjerg's theory of expertise. Here we turn to the notion of professional learning communities. While there is no universal definition of a professional learning community, they are usually depicted as a situation in which people involved with and concerned about schooling work collaboratively to learn about how they can improve pupil learning or outcomes. For example, such communities have been described by Stoll as a means through which to build 'learning [in order] to support educational improvement' (Stoll, 2008: 107). Stoll continues by suggesting that professional learning communities comprise: 'inclusive, reflective, mutually supportive and collaborative groups of people who find ways, inside and outside their immediate community, to investigate and learn more about their practice' (Stoll, 2008: 107). The notion of professional learning communities thus encapsulates instances where practitioners and researchers might come together in order to facilitate learning about and from formalized/academic knowledge.

Importantly, a key benefit of the professional learning communities approach may be attributed to the nature of the learning that takes place within them, which is encapsulated by the process of knowledge 'creation'. This is described by Stoll (2008) (who uses the term 'animation') as a process whereby the producers and users of formal knowledge, who are respectively also the users and holders of 'practical' knowledge, come together to create 'new' knowledge. Activities to facilitate knowledge-creation are considered in detail in Stoll (2009) – and in Chapter 5 – and we outline our approach in a general sense below.

The Camden Early Years Learning Community project

Educational provision for children under 5 in England is offered within a range of diverse settings including nursery classes, private and voluntary nurseries, children's centres, and primary schools. Historically, the fragmented and patchy nature of this provision has created difficulties and divisions for children, their families, and practitioners alike. To achieve greater coherence in provision the Early Years Foundation Stage (EYFS) was established in 2008 and revised in 2012.[2] The EYFS was devised with the following aims:

- setting the standards for children's learning, development, and care from birth to statutory school age at 5
- improving quality and consistency in the early years sector
- laying a secure foundation for future learning through individual learning and development planned around the individual needs and interests of the child
- providing equality of opportunity
- creating the framework for partnership working.

(Department for Education, 2012)

The qualifications of staff working with young children are highly variable and match the diversity of provision in the sector. Latest figures suggest that 73 per cent of staff working in childcare settings are qualified to Level 3, the equivalent of an A Level in England. A much lower figure of 7 per cent is qualified to Level 6, or graduate level. In nursery and reception classes within primary schools the figure for graduate-level qualification is higher, with around 40 per cent having qualified teacher status (Department for Education, 2012). Considerable progress has been made to improve the qualifications of those working with young children. A further challenge, however, is that of continuing professional development in a period of significant change in the policy landscape and in curricular and pedagogical requirements. For example, it is now widely accepted that good pedagogical leadership makes a difference to the quality of early years provision, particularly with regard to implementing the EYFS via the provision of an enabling environment and, critically, an enabling pedagogy that meets the complex learning needs of children in the early years (Rogers, 2014).

Against this background, the Camden project responded to a specific identified need to improve the skills and knowledge of a diverse group of practitioners in relation to the requirements of the EYFS. In particular, Camden Local Authority and a number of heads of early years settings in the borough argued that support was required with regard to the newly introduced 'Characteristics of effective learning', which provide the context for learning in the EYFS. These are:

- playing and exploring – children investigate and experience things, and 'have a go'
- active learning – children concentrate and keep trying if they encounter difficulties
- creating and thinking critically – children have and develop their own ideas, make links between ideas, and develop strategies for doing things.

(Department for Education, 2012)

The main objectives of the community therefore were to improve outcomes both for children and for adults by:

- increasing practitioners' understanding of and confidence in using the newly introduced 'Characteristics of effective learning'
- enhancing early years practitioners' teaching skills, particularly in promoting children's 'Creating and thinking critically' characteristic (i.e. children's ability to 'have their own ideas', 'make links', and 'choose ways to do things'): this focus was informed by research evidence indicating that this characteristic is linked to self-regulation, creativity, and motivation (Whitebread *et al.*, 2009)
- developing a *sustainable* model of practitioner development and partnership that will support children's learning, particularly those in disadvantaged groups.

In order to realize these objectives, the authors established a professional learning community comprising 36 practitioners from 18 early years settings from within Camden who were keen to take advantage of the opportunity for developing their skills in this way.

The aim of the learning community was to assist participating practitioners (two from each setting) in developing a wider repertoire of interactive strategies that better support children's creative and critical thinking. It was envisaged that such strategies would be formed from a combination of external (academic) evidence and practitioners' own understanding of best practice, and that the enactment of these strategies would be observed, critiqued, and improved upon via a process of facilitated lesson study throughout the year. The effectiveness of these strategies in meeting their objectives (in terms of practitioners' and children's outcomes) was established via an evaluation process where baseline data were collected at the beginning of the project, intermediary data were collected at monthly intervals, and endline (outcome) data were collected at the project's 12-month conclusion. At the same time the authors sought to use the evaluation process as, first, a means of testing the learning-community approach as a way of facilitating evidence-informed practice and, second, as a way of measuring practitioners' 'state' of being evidence-informed.

Our approach to knowledge creation

A knowledge-creation workshop was held during the inaugural professional learning community meeting. Following Nonaka and Takeuchi (1995) and Stoll (2009), this involved researchers facilitating a discussion that at first centred on current academic evidence and knowledge (both theoretical and empirical) in relation to effective early years practice. (This process had been constructed via a literature review that was specifically undertaken for the project). Practitioners were then invited to share their own practical knowledge, for example, data and insight about their settings and current practices, via exercises designed to surface this knowledge. They were subsequently invited to establish what they wanted to achieve by the end of the project and how they might do so. Specifically, following an approach set out by Earley and Porritt (2014) and 'starting with the end in mind' (the goal they wished to achieve), practitioners were asked how they might use academic knowledge presented to them, their own practical knowledge, and knowledge provided by others in their study group, to produce strategies to reach this end-point.

Following this initial workshop, practitioners from the 18 partner settings were paired into six groups of three. Each setting hosted one visit per term for their study group. During each visit, each of these study groups (and a facilitator) spent the morning of their session in the setting observing a specific lesson undertaken by the host practitioner. Before the lesson, the host practitioner briefed the observing practitioners on what they wanted to achieve and on the desired outcomes. In the afternoon the group reflected on the 'success' of the lesson and offered suggestions for how it might be improved, as well as planning the next lesson study.

In order to ensure research evidence remained 'top of mind', the facilitators were asked to ensure that, as well as improvements grounded in practitioner knowledge, they prompted for potential improvements suggested by the research. They did this through the use of non-specific questions, for example by asking things such as 'how might we incorporate what we know from the research here?' At the end of each lesson study day, all 36 participating practitioners came together for a seminar hosted by an early years research 'expert' (the second author) to ensure that learning was shared and reflected upon across the group. Where pertinent, the research expert would relate practitioner experiences shared during the feedback session to the research presented (i.e. to specific theories, approaches, and authors).

Measuring evidence use

Our first approach to measuring evidence use saw us draw upon a study successfully undertaken by Landry *et al.* (2003), and used the following descriptor terms:

1. *Reception:* the research was well communicated
2. *Cognition:* I understood the findings of the research
3. *Discussion:* I discussed with others within my study group how the research might be used
4. *Reference:* I could relate the research findings to my setting
5. *Effort:* I used the research in subsequent exercises (when thinking about the approaches I might use in my setting)
6. *Influence:* I intend to apply/have applied the research as part of my approach.

In order to collect data against our scale, a self-completion survey was employed at the end of the knowledge-creation workshop. Specifically, respondents were asked to consider all six elements and indicate the extent to which they agreed using a five-point scale, which ranged from 'strongly agree' to 'strongly disagree'. In total 33 of 36 participants completed the survey.

Levels of use

While our first scale appeared to be useful for assessing the effectiveness of the knowledge-creation activity as a means of communicating research, we also needed to determine whether the level of expertise of practitioners' use of evidence increased over time. As a result, our second approach to measuring evidence use involved a revised version of the Levels of Use scale developed by Hall and Hord (2001) as part of their wider work in developing the Concerns-Based Adoption Model (CBAM). The Levels of Use scale represents eight classifications relating to how people act or behave in response to a newly introduced change or innovation. Specifically, it reflects the observation that, as with the notion of expertise, just because an innovation has been suggested or mandated, it does not mean that it will necessarily be implemented, or that all individuals will employ the innovation in the same way. Some users may 'stumble along', while others use the innovation to achieve groundbreaking ends. Figure 6.1 relates the Flyvbjerg expertise scale and the Hall and Hord Levels of Use scale.

Hall and Hord	Flyvbjerg expertise	New typology and descriptors based on Hall and Hord and seeking to elicit expertise
Non-use	Non-use	NON-USE: I haven't attempted to use any of the findings from the research within my day-to-day practice.
Orientation	Non-use	ORIENTATION: I have begun to consider how to use some of the findings of the research as part of my day-to-day practice, for example in terms of specific strategies suggested by the research.
Preparation	Non-use to Novice	PREPARATION: I have made concrete plans to use some of the research findings as part of my day-to-day practice and am waiting for the opportunity to do so.
Mechanical use	Novice to Advanced beginner	NOVICE: I have now begun to implement specific strategies suggested by the research within my day-to-day practice.
Routine	Competent	COMPETENT: I now regularly use some of the research findings within my day-to-day practice. For example I frequently use specific strategies suggested by the research.
Refinement	Proficient	PROFICIENT: I have begun to tailor my use of the research findings so that I can incorporate other aspects of effective practice that I know about.
Integration to Renewal	Proficient to Expert	PROFICIENT +: I regularly adapt the strategies suggested by the research in order to make them even more effective or so that they can apply to a number of situations within my setting.
-	Expert	EXPERT: I frequently use the research strategies we learnt about but I now incorporate them into my day-to-day practice in an automatic rather than conscious way, as I tackle specific situations and issues.

Figure 6.1: Typologies and descriptors of expertise: The 'expertise in evidence use' scale

Again, respondents were asked to consider all eight elements and to indicate the extent to which they agreed with them using a scale that ranged from 'strongly agree' to 'strongly disagree'. The survey was administered in December 2013, some four months after the beginning of the project. In total 34 of 36 participants completed the survey.

Findings

Beginning with results from our first scale, it can be seen in Table 6.1 that all respondents agreed or strongly agreed that the research was well communicated (stage 1); comprehension (stage 2) was also high, with 94 per cent agreeing or strongly agreeing that they understood what had been communicated (no respondents disagreed or strongly disagreed with this statement). This pattern continues until stage 4 of the ladder ('I can see how the research related to my setting'), where 3 per cent disagree; correspondingly, this same 3 per cent disagreed that they felt that they had started to use the research in subsequent exercises (stage 5) or had any intention of using the research moving forward (stage 6). Conversely, 97 per cent suggested that they had actively discussed the research presented (stage 3); 94 per cent could see its relevance and had discussed the research in the exercises throughout the day (stages 4 and 5); and 97 per cent expressed the intention to use findings as they developed approaches and strategies for their setting (stage 6).

Table 6.1: Findings from scale 1 (n=33)

Stage	Strongly disagree (%)	Disagree (%)	Neither (%)	Agree (%)	Strongly agree (%)	Total (%)
Reception	–	–	–	58	42	100
Cognition	–	–	6	61	33	100
Discussion	–	–	3	70	27	100
Reference	–	3	3	49	45	100
Effort	–	3	3	63	31	100
Influence	–	3	–	45	52	100

Expertise in evidence use scale

Findings from our 'expertise in evidence use scale' are presented in Table 6.2. As can be seen, and as might be expected after four months of activity, the majority of respondents (94 per cent) indicated that they had made attempts to use at least some of the research presented as part of their day-to-day practice. Following this, however (and again, as might be expected, assuming that generally there will be fewer people at the highest levels of expertise), there is a steady decline in the percentage of respondents agreeing or strongly agreeing with the statements regarding positive research use. This decline finally culminates in only one third of participants scoring themselves as experts.

In more detail, it can be seen that as we progress through the questions 94 per cent agree or strongly agree that their use was around 'orientation' – considering how research findings might be implemented. The level of agreement falls to 76 per cent for 'preparation' – making plans to use findings. Two thirds (65 per cent) suggest they are 'proficient' – beginning to tailor the research findings so that they are contextually appropriate. At the highest levels of expertise only 47 per cent agreed (no one strongly agreed) that they were regularly adapting the strategies suggested by the research in order to make them even more effective ('proficient +'). Finally, only 35 per cent agreed (no one strongly agreed) with the statement relating to full expertise: 'I have used the research strategies we learnt about so often now that I barely need to even think about them, they've just become part of my day-to-day practice.'

Table 6.2: Findings by typology, derived from the combined Expertise and Levels of Use scale (n=34)

Descriptor	Strongly disagree (%)	Disagree (%)	Neither (%)	Agree (%)	Strongly agree (%)	Total (%)
Non-use	35	53	6	–	6	100
Orientation	6	–	–	88	6	100
Preparation	–	12	12	64	12	100
Novice	–	–	29	59	12	100
Competent	–	6	19	62	13	100
Proficient	–	–	35	53	12	100
Proficient +	–	12	41	47	–	100
Expert	6	12	47	35	–	100

Interview data

Due to the Christmas break, interviews were held almost two months after the 'expertise in evidence use scale' survey was administered. Participants were re-issued with the survey to remind them of its contents and were also reminded of their responses. Interestingly, while agreeing that, theoretically at least, expertise in evidence use might build over time, the length of gap between completion and interview also meant that some respondents were able to identify changes in their behaviour: 'just looking through the questions again, I can see plenty now that I wouldn't have been able to [tick 'agree' on] before' (interviewee #6). For example, those at the lower end of the scale were now revisiting in detail the research that was introduced at the beginning of the project. Often this was part of an overall process of sharing new pedagogic approaches with colleagues: 'we've run a whole INSET day to show staff what we've found ... and demonstrate some of the new approaches that have emerged' (interviewee #2).

Others, when asked if they felt they might reach the level of expertise implied by the top end of the scale, suggested that they believed they were now 'getting there' (interviewee #4). For example, one noted: 'when we are engaged in the activities, I now think to myself "don't rush" and that, thinking about it, was something that came as a result of listening to the research and in discussing how to do this with the study group ... it [the research] just comes to me straight away now' (interviewee #5). Others discussed the strategies developed within the study group as becoming 'second nature' (interviewee #1). As a result, because they could now relate this type of change to their actual behaviour, respondents felt strongly that the scale reflected how expertise in using evidence as part of practice develops over time.

Conclusion

This chapter presents an initial attempt to establish ways of measuring: (1) meaningful evidence use – defined as the result of combining external and practitioner evidence such that this leads to expertise; and (2) the effectiveness of knowledge-creation activity as a means of establishing meaningful evidence use. Based on the results of the two surveys outlined above, our findings would appear to be encouraging. Not only does knowledge-creation activity provide an effective way of communicating evidence and keeping it 'top of mind', it also seems to enable practitioners to develop expertise in using evidence by helping them combine external evidence with practice-based or tacit understanding in practical ways. Simultaneously our interview data appear to triangulate and verify the trustworthiness of measures used in the surveys as a way of measuring levels of expertise in evidence use.

Take-out messages

- **TAKE-OUT** ①: Being evidence informed is not about the mechanical implementation of science; it is about building on what we know (both in terms of academic and practice-based knowledge) in order to perform better.
- **TAKE-OUT** ②: To achieve expertise in evidence use requires practitioners to learn both about their own evidence, and about that produced by others. This can be achieved in effective learning environments such as professional learning communities, which, through the use of knowledge-creation activity, enable practitioners to combine evidence and create new knowledge pertinent to their setting.
- **TAKE-OUT** ③: Learning must move beyond 'theoretical' learning; however, proposed solutions based on external evidence must be tested and modelled. In other words, potential solutions must be practised in real-life settings and refined so that practitioners know exactly when and how they should be deployed.
- **TAKE-OUT** ④: Leaders facilitating learning, and also supporting practitioners in taking (reasonable) risks in trialling new strategies, are a vital aspect of developing evidence-informed schools.

Endnotes

[1] These levels are (1) 'novice'; (2) 'advanced beginner'; (3) 'competent performer'; (4) 'proficient performer'; and (5) 'expert'.

[2] See www.gov.uk/government/policies/improving-the-quality-and-range-of-education-and-childcare-from-birth-to-5-years/supporting-pages/early-years-foundation-stage (accessed 17 February 2014).

References

Brown, C. (2013) *Making Evidence Matter: A new perspective for evidence-informed policy making in education*. London: Institute of Education Press.

— (2014) *Evidence-Informed Policy and Practice in Education: A sociological grounding*. London: Bloomsbury.

Department for Children, Schools and Families (2010) *Parenting and Family Support: Guidance for loal authorities in England*. Online. http://webarchive.nationalarchives.gov.uk/20130401151715/http://www.education.gov.uk/publications/eOrderingDownload/DCSF-00264-2010.PDF (accessed 12 February 2015).

Department for Education (2012) 'Early Years Foundation Stage Framework 2012'. Online. www.gov.uk/government/uploads/system/uploads/attachment_data/file/271631/eyfs_statutory_framework_march_2012.pdf (accessed 8 July 2012).

Earley, P., and Porritt, V. (2014) 'Evaluating the impact of professional development: The need for a student-focused approach'. *Professional Development in Education*, 40 (1), 112–29.

Flyvbjerg, B. (2001) *Making Social Science Matter: Why social inquiry fails and how it can succeed again.* Cambridge: Cambridge University Press.

Hall, G.E., and Hord, S.M. (2001) *Implementing Change: Patterns, principles and potholes.* Boston: Allyn and Bacon.

Landry, R., Lamari, M., and Amara, N. (2003) 'The extent and determinants of the utilization of university research in government agencies'. *Public Administration Review*, 63 (2), 192–-205.

Nonaka, I., and Takeuchi, H. (1995) *The Knowledge-Creating Company: How Japanese companies create the dynamics of innovation.* New York: Oxford University Press.

Rogers, S. (2014) 'Enabling pedagogy: Meanings and practices'. In Moyles, J., Payler, J., and Georgeson, J. (eds) *Early Years Foundations: Critical issues.* Maidenhead: Open University Press 41–51.

Stoll, L. (2008) 'Leadership and policy learning communities: Promoting knowledge animation'. In Chakroun, B., and Sahlberg, P. (eds) *European Training Foundation Yearbook 2008: Policy learning in action.* Luxembourg: European Training Foundation/Office for Official Publications of the European Communities, 107–12.

— (2009) 'Knowledge animation in policy and practice: Making connections'. Paper presented at the Annual Meeting of the American Educational Research Association as part of the symposium 'Using Knowledge to Change Policy and Practice', San Diego, CA. 13–17 April. Online. http://www.researchgate.net/publication/254804117_Knowledge_Animation_in_Policy_and_Practice_Making_Connections (accessed 25 January 2015).

Whitebread, D., Coltman, P., Pasternak, D.P., Sangster, C., Grau, V., Bingham, S., Almeqdad, Q., and Demetriou, D. (2009) 'The development of two observational tools for assessing metacognition and self-regulated learning in young children'. *Metacognition and Learning*, 4 (1), 63–85.

Chapter 7

Leading 'disciplined enquiries' in schools
Hélène Galdin-O'Shea

> Every teacher needs to improve, not because they are not good enough, but because they can be even better.
>
> Dylan Wiliam

Chapter overview

School practitioners require support in leading their own enquiries. This chapter identifies different ways in which teachers lead different kinds of enquiry in their own school settings and across Teaching School Alliances, and the support they require for this process. It also looks at specific case studies, identifying a range of models, and acknowledges the fact that 'practitioner research' is a very broad phrase used to refer to many things, from teachers engaging 'with' research to action research projects engaging 'in' research. The chapter will also examine issues that need to be overcome to create a successful professional learning community.

Introduction

There are many reasons not only why teachers should be encouraged to lead their own enquiries and become engaged with research, but also why our schools' culture must change to allow this to happen in a meaningful way.

The Sutton Trust report, *Improving the Impact of Teachers on Pupil Achievement in the UK* (2011), makes it clear that:

> The effects of high-quality teaching are especially significant for pupils from disadvantaged backgrounds: over a school year, these pupils gain 1.5 years' worth of learning with very effective teachers, compared with 0.5 years with poorly performing teachers. In other words, for poor pupils the difference between a good teacher and a bad teacher is a whole year's learning.
>
> (Sutton Trust, 2011: 2)

The figures are convincing. The economic argument is also important and is made both in the Sutton Trust report and by Dylan Wiliam, who argues that 'the educational achievement of a country's population is a key determinant of economic growth, and so improving educational attainment is an urgent priority for all countries.' (Wiliam, 2011: no page numbers)

Wiliam also makes the point that for decades Continuing Professional Development (CPD) has attempted to solve a deficit in teacher knowledge by filling in 'missing information', but he adds:

> Changes in what teachers know or believe will not benefit students unless teachers also change what they do in classrooms. We have been focusing on getting teachers to think their way into a new way of acting, whereas it would be far more effective to get teachers to act their way into a new way of thinking.
>
> (Wiliam, 2010: no page numbers)

He also warns that changing habits, or teacher behaviours, in the classroom is hard because it is a difficult process to change the way that you do things after a long time. Wiliam says that the key idea for improving teachers' practice is 'the realization that we need to help teachers change habits rather than acquire new knowledge'. He adds that teachers need 'small steps as they develop their practice', that they need to be 'accountable for developing their practice', and that 'they need to be given support for change' (Wiliam, 2010: no page numbers).

We also know that in the UK, variability at classroom level is often four times greater than variability between schools. In view of this, focus on improvement within our own classrooms is an imperative. Furthermore, we know that for CPD to impact our teaching, and therefore to have any impact on students' outcomes, it needs to be personalized, reflective, sustained, iterative, collaborative, focused, and constantly evaluated and reviewed. It should also take into consideration our own local contexts. There is now substantial evidence, for example in the British Educational Research Association/ Royal Society for the Encouragement of Arts, Manufacturing and Commerce report, *Improving the Impact of Teachers on Pupil Achievement in the UK* (2014), that:

> ... research has a major contribution to make to effective teacher education in a whole variety of different ways. There is also some robust evidence that doing so improves the quality of students' learning in schools.
>
> (The British Educational Research Association/
> The Royal Society for the Encouragement of Arts,
> Manufacturing and Commerce, 2014: 4)

With all this in mind, many schools have started to engage in different forms of teacher-led enquiries and action research. This is a complicated process as many barriers get in the way, but it is a rewarding one, for both staff and students.

What is practitioner research?

Practitioner research can encompass several pursuits, and can even be called different things, from action research to practitioner-led enquiry. Many schools are currently adopting lesson study as a way of conducting some of this research. For some, engaging *with* research in the form of reading and then distilling the knowledge gained through their own practice in a methodical and systematic way is an enriching starting point. Such research usually puts participants at the heart of the study.

It is worth mentioning some of the difficulties that schools face if they truly want to establish a culture in which teachers feel supported in their professional development. Most of these difficulties occur at a system level. Lack of time is the first factor mentioned by teachers. It takes time for meaningful professional dialogue to occur, for example during a cycle of action research. Lack of time is often related to a lack of clear leadership, or a weak commitment to allow a culture of support to flourish, to make it a real priority. This can too often be compounded by a thousand initiatives which overburden teachers who are often already working at full capacity. It takes a brave leader indeed to recognize that the impact of all these initiatives is often limited, if evaluated at all, and that the biggest factor leading to improved students' outcomes is the quality of the teaching that takes place every day.

Another barrier to creating a thriving learning teacher community that has to be acknowledged is the fact that some teachers are reluctant to engage. In many cases this is understandable, as many teachers have seen initiatives come and go, and have often been subjected to years of poor CPD that was lacking in continuity and that was unlikely to have made an impact on their teaching. It is important to secure teacher buy-in, but it is also important not to give up too quickly. Changing a school culture takes time, and as we will see from the case studies I outline below, it often takes several attempts before an ethos of self-improvement and research-informed enquiry can be truly achieved. Even partial success leads to a more successful cycle the next time around.

Park High School: Teacher-led enquiries and lesson study, or 'How to learn some hard lessons'

At Park High School, the CPD provision had already managed to engage staff in collaborative and cross-curricular, cross-experience triads some years ago, with some degree of success. In 2013 staff were asked to lead their own enquiries and were offered more autonomy in their choice of groups and topics. Park High's approach to enquiry is set out in *resource box 7.1*.

RESOURCE BOX 7.1:

Park High's enquiry approach was set out to staff in the following way:

- decide why you are doing this – what specific area of the curriculum or of your teaching would you like to focus on?
- decide who will benefit, how they will benefit, and how you will know
- decide what you are not going to do instead – what strategies/ initiatives will you discard and why?
- dig into the theory and research
- collaborate, try, reflect, evaluate – accountability to self and peers
- gather a portfolio of evidence to document the process; focus on outcomes
- beware groupthink; find some challenge
- embed and disseminate!
- encourage further research into a question by formulating related questions that have not been addressed or answered yet.

Also provided was an 'Evaluation Guidance Template' (see the chapter appendix).

It was suggested that groups made up of colleagues from the same department might be a good starting point, thereby tapping into teachers' wishes to focus their professional development on an area of their own curriculum. Teacher feedback from the previous cycle had mentioned the need for more time to develop and consolidate strategies, and to plan collaboratively *within departments*, along with the need to share and *embed* good practice. There was also a feeling that some of the CPD offer lacked coherence and that staff had a preference for in-depth expertise on an area of their practice rather than sound bites and strategies that are rarely embedded. The staff's

CPD wish list also included: more time; more peer lesson observations – developmental, not high stakes; a differentiated CPD offer; sessions where independent reading, including research, would be offered (this was not a feeling shared by all but it was noted several times).

The philosophy which underpinned professional development was to: move away from focusing on what makes an 'Outstanding' lesson, Ofsted-approved[1] or otherwise; to foster collaborative work and coaching; to focus on pupils' learning rather than on what the teacher is doing at the front; to encourage and implement evaluation of the interventions' impact on students' learning; to create the right conditions for teachers to thrive in, and for their work to become more research-informed; and for teachers to be more researched-engaged. Some of Park High School's more practical considerations are set out in *resource box 7.2*.

RESOURCE BOX 7.2:

Park High School allocated nine CPD sessions, taking place from 4 to 5 p.m., which would be used for teacher-led enquiries. Teachers organized themselves into groups, each focused on one enquiry question. Clusters of groups were organized, working on related topics, and linked to a mentor who would steer discussions and remind groups of deadlines, act as a supportive voice as well as a critical friend, forward relevant reading, and generally facilitate the groups' work. Most of the mentors were also part of an enquiry group themselves. In many cases, lesson study was used as a tool to further the enquiries.

One of the exciting aspects of this approach was in thinking about ways in which what we do is evaluated, and to design the enquiry with the evaluation in mind. For many teachers, this was indeed an obstacle and it quickly became obvious that teachers need support and training on this. A range of evaluation sources was mentioned, such as formative and summative assessments; quality of homework and classwork including participation; teachers' own observations supported by notes and photographs of work produced, and possibly videos of the lessons, or parts of lessons; team members' observations; post-lesson (and possibly pre-lesson) interviews with focus pupils; other statistics such as attendance and punctuality figures; comments in contact books; and so on. All this was further supported by a planning sheet with questions aimed at breaking down each stage in more detail.

An invaluable document is the EEF *DIY Evaluation Guide* produced by Professor Robert Coe and Stuart Kime from Durham University, and freely available at http://educationendowmentfoundation. org.uk/toolkit/.

One very successful group, from the PE department, looked at a very concrete problem. GCSE[2] students were getting very few marks on one specific type of question in their exam. The group's final enquiry question was: 'How can we get students to gain more marks in the 8-mark questions in the AQA[3] GCSE Physical Education written paper?' While some might consider this question to be very narrowly focused, and others might worry that it encourages a 'teach to the test' approach, the resulting journey was absolutely fascinating. It involved gathering data at both school level and national level, deconstructing students' answers, interviewing students throughout the process, creating and evaluating a range of resources, discarding the least effective ones, and gathering resources from beyond the school.

Students were actively involved in the evaluation process, and this in itself sharpened their focus. By the end of the year, the teachers felt that they had really developed their expertise in this area of the curriculum. After one activity in which students were asked to colour-code their responses, one teacher commented that 'students were able to visually see where they had gained marks and areas they needed to improve'. One student noted that 'it was very helpful though shocking to me to see how much waffle I had included in my response'. The GCSE results also confirmed that the work undertaken had produced significantly higher marks on that question.

Lesson study was the tool used in many, but not all, of the enquiries. The range of enquiry questions was wide and included: 'How effective is diagnostic marking between students and teachers and does it have an impact on their learning or attainment?'; 'How can we strengthen the knowledge retrieval capacity of our students? (Beating the 'I can't remember' line)'; 'How can we change the perception of computer science and IT to encourage more girls to choose this subject for further study?' Further information on lesson study can be found in *resource box 7.3*.

RESOURCE BOX 7.3:
For those whose enquiry lent itself to lesson study, the approach recommended by the National Teacher Enquiry Network (NTEN)[4] was shared. The process is as follows:

1. the set up: choose an enquiry question or learning goal; design your evaluation; investigate the issue and get a baseline
2. the enquiry through lesson study: plan and try an intervention; interim review and expert input/research; refine your intervention
3. complete your evaluation: write up your evaluation and summary report; share and disseminate.

Stage 2 can be looped to gather more evidence and continue to refine the intervention.

The lesson study cycle itself adopts the following pattern:

1. Plan: Plan a lesson together, address each activity to your learning goal and predict how pupils will react and how you will assess this. Pick three case pupils.
2. Observe: Teach the lesson with your colleagues observing. Pay particular attention to the case pupils. Pay attention to pupils rather than the teacher.
3. Conduct any assessments and interviews during and after.
4. Reflect and plan: As soon after the lesson as possible, reflect on how each activity elicited the sought-after change. Were your predictions correct and why?

Lesson Study websites, with a wealth of resources and guidance, include:

- http://lessonstudy.co.uk/
- http://scittls.weebly.com/
- http://leicls.weebly.com/uploads/9/6/0/1/9601453/ses_lesson_study_report.pdf
- www.meolscophighschool.co.uk/dep-blog/?cat=8

Final reports were produced and stored and groups presented their work at the end of the year through a 'Carousel of Enquiries', which was positively received even though it probably happened too late in the summer term. The point is that any school attempting this type of engagement in and with research needs to accept that not everything will be perfect the first time around. A first 'run' is undoubtedly about learning how to do it, and about getting staff to view their professional development in a new and proactive way. It is the leadership's responsibility to ensure that subsequent cycles run more smoothly.

Coming up with an enquiry question: A big ask

The first hurdle is for a group to come up with an enquiry question that is relevant, focused, and offers scope for an enquiry. The task of coming up with an interesting enquiry question is a challenge in itself, but it produces rich professional dialogue. The focus has to be on something that will genuinely move teaching forward and impact positively on students' outcomes. Many of the initial questions were later refined or changed after discussion. Some of the issues are interesting and worth noting here.

Firstly, there is the question of whether to make the enquiry one of the Performance Management targets. Some departments took this approach and high-quality work was produced as a result. The concern is, however, that some heads of departments could steer the discussion too far towards what *they* would wish to see as a target. There has to be autonomy in the choice of focus so that teachers feel that they are the drivers of their own development. Keeping this philosophy in mind (in other words 'done with, not done to'), the process works. Of course it is likely that enquiries will need to fall within an area of the school or departmental development plan, but this should generally be broad enough to allow for scope within the enquiries. The approach to enquiries should not be too prescriptive, and some may argue that this should not be a factor at all. Treating teachers as professionals has to remain the imperative.

Secondly, at Park High School some questions had to be redrafted after initial planning when it became obvious that it would be difficult to gather evidence, or when it appeared that the focus was too broad, or too narrow, to make a significant impact on students' outcomes. This is another issue that has to be tackled: we know that most interventions will have *some* impact, but with limited time and resources, it is important to consider which interventions will have more impact than other available strategies. This has to be given time for discussion, but what rich discussion! However, it is probably unrealistic to think that all enquiries will achieve their maximum potential effectiveness. Things are likely to get better year-on-year as teachers become more used to this way of tackling professional development, and the research methods they use are likely to improve too, particularly if support and training are offered along the way. It is also important to make sure that the research conducted is shared and stored, including the work of colleagues who have completed master's degrees, because cumulating research has to be an essential component of a whole staff's developmental journey. This is something that is lacking in most schools, but something that a Research Lead within a school or across a Teaching School Alliance could facilitate.

Thirdly, for hard-pressed teachers it is perhaps tempting simply to choose an area of focus that they know is the 'flavour du jour' for Senior Leadership Teams (SLTs), or a teaching fad that is currently being pushed from above, such as Triple impact marking or dialogic marking. It is easy to see why this might happen, and it raises another interesting point: you do not know what you do not know. How can an individual or small group investigate an area of pedagogy that they have little or no knowledge about? Some of the feedback at the end of the year suggested that more upfront input would have been helpful. Once again, this raises questions: how can you open up enough investigative paths without steering the directions of enquiries too much? Who makes the decisions? How do you avoid confirmation biases? How do you make sure that the direction of enquiry is genuinely a priority for all individuals in the triad/group?

There is always the risk of one teacher leading the thinking and/or imposing their own biases on the group, along with a risk of 'groupthink' being established with little to challenge it. The answer, as ever, is to treat staff as professionals and to trust them to be aware of the risks. It is something that must be acknowledged from the start, and a culture of challenging each other, acting as 'critical friends', and actively looking for contradictory views and evidence must be encouraged. To facilitate this, the need for a central place in which to store a wealth of evidence-informed starting points, research resources, papers, and reflections quickly becomes obvious. It also follows that when evidence is gathered, leadership must be prepared to be challenged if they are promoting another direction of travel. At some point, there has to be expert input. The phrase itself is not without problems: what do we mean by 'expert input' and how do we go about finding it, internally and externally?

John Henry Newman Catholic College: Refining the process and overcoming some of the barriers identified

At John Henry Newman Catholic College (JHNCC), previous action research cycles have informed the implementation of the latest format and, borrowing a phrase from Dylan Wiliam again, they are now talking about 'disciplined enquiry' to describe the developmental work in which teachers are engaged. The vision is clearly about using enquiry research methods to investigate the impact of the planning, initiatives, and developments into which staff pour their energy. In fact, they now use the term *CPrD* to emphasize the research-informed nature of their work.

Having opted for a meeting-light calendar, after-school CPD sessions now have a tight focus on supporting groups' enquiries. Now in the fourth year of the process, some hard lessons have been learnt and the format has been tweaked to allow staff more autonomy in terms of groupings and choice of focus. At the same time, the supporting structure is much more rigorous and cleverly designed to allow more in-depth and robustly evaluated types of enquiries. As with Park High, staff commitment and engagement was inconsistent in previous cycles, and it was clear that CPD had to be made everyone's responsibility. It had to be made obvious that it should not be an 'add-on' to the day job, but a crucial part of it. In fact, staff engaged in conducting their master's degrees should use the cycle as an authentic part of their course.

Staff are also getting more expert at conducting their own research and the buy-in is more easily achieved in the light of past successes and positive outcomes for students. The enquiry cycles have also become longer and, interestingly, there are now fewer formal group meetings but better outcomes.

Another essential component was to secure the support of external expertise to overview the process and conduct a parallel evaluation of it. The school enlisted the help of 'Research Partners', including a link with the University of Leicester. Dr Phil Wood agreed to present to staff in one of the initial sessions about how best to take research and literature into the classroom, and to then help develop enquiries to be more academic and to make the work produced more shareable for colleagues at school and beyond. Some of the more practical considerations from JHNCC's approach are set out in *resource box 7.4*.

RESOURCE BOX 7.4:

Key to JHNCC's success has been the format of the designated meetings, with a combination of planned input and time for groups to work on their projects, for example:

- Before the first meeting, staff were informed, via email and morning briefings, about how the process had evolved. They were asked to form their groups and chose their focus ahead of the meeting. This made for a much more productive meeting during which not only were the process and some of the methods to be used clearly articulated, but groups were also given time to discuss and refine their enquiries.

- Two successful groups from the previous cycles presented their work, mainly to showcase what could be achieved but also for the benefit of new staff.
- Dr Wood presented at the second meeting, highlighting the core purpose of research in education, how universities use it, and how teachers could also harness it.
- Groups had been asked to bring initial relevant research to feed into their discussions. They were given six questions to help them shape their project and build in the evaluation processes to be used. A Google document was created to allow each group to keep a diary of developments, with specific input points for specific deadlines.

To support the enquiries further, e-bulletins were circulated with links to relevant research for the topics chosen. The spring term will see the groups ready to start implementing the interventions and two sessions are planned to support the process and guide staff through the evaluative dimension of the projects, while still allowing time for group discussion, specifically for looking at what the data are showing and what can be learnt from them. Groups will also be preparing for the writing of the report and the presentation of the findings at the end of the cycle. There will be a hiatus during the exam preparation season, something that staff asked to be taken into consideration in the previous cycle, then the sharing and disseminating will happen at the end of the summer term.

As in previous cycles, Friday morning briefings are dedicated to showcasing the ongoing work of groups, with short presentations from group members. A website is being developed to gather resources, advice, and contributions from the enquiry groups.

It is worth noting that as with Park High, SLT members are also involved in leading their own enquiries, something that is crucial if the message is to permeate the fabric of the school. They have also offered to cover for colleagues to allow for peer observation of research lessons to take place. The notion of accountability is important: it was made clear to teachers that once they sign up to a group and topic, it becomes their responsibility to commit to the process and see it through.

Cramlington Learning Village: Prioritizing CPD

In the case of the two schools discussed above, time for staff to conduct their enquiries had to be found, but the solutions were not necessarily ideal. At Park High, in fact, it was clear that the slot at the end of the day was far from ideal; nonetheless this is a regular meeting slot and action research meetings were integral to the cycle. At JHNCC, on the other hand, there are few timetabled meetings, and yet creative ways of providing time is essential for the work to happen and for the enquiries not to feel like an extra burden. It is undeniable that the effort required to conduct and sustain an enquiry over time is more demanding than simply attending one-off CPD sessions (rendering the C in CPD rather redundant). It goes without saying that the most important way to signal that staff professional development is important is to remove as many barriers as possible, and to create workable windows for teachers to collaborate. True support and vision from the top means that ways must be found to do this. Some schools have shortened some of their lunchtimes in order to fit in a timetabled CPD session at the end of the day. While there are obvious advantages to having regular slots, schools need to consider carefully what the impact of these choices will be on the rest of the week for both pupils and staff.

Cramlington is an interesting case. Their CPD provision is something of which they are rightly proud, and they have taken the brave decision to create a weekly CPD slot. On Wednesdays, the 'teaching day' finishes early to allow for directed CPD time. Students go home early and staff can engage in professional dialogue and developmental activities for two hours. Part of the provision is to use some of this time for Professional Enquiry Groups. All teaching staff join an enquiry group of their choice and follow this interest for the whole year, with groups meeting half termly. Staff undertake their own classroom-based action research projects and share their findings with the whole staff via *The Muse* (an online publication used for sharing effective practice within and beyond Cramlington[5]) and showcases. Once again, the philosophy behind giving staff autonomy for their projects is to empower teachers as 'change agents'. A facilitator is appointed to lead each group, and staff choose an area in which they are interested and devise their own line of enquiry. Staff then produce an academic poster and host a round table to share impact.

As with the other schools mentioned above, the quality of the work produced has increased with each cycle, but the ultimate question of evaluating the impact on students' outcomes remains a focus. Teaming up with the National Teacher Enquiry Network (NTEN)[6] and Sheffield Hallam

University brought about some forward steps. Their CPD R&D project is now leading the way. They secured funding through the National Research and Development Network[7] and, in conjunction with other schools within their Teaching School Alliance (TSA) and the support of the university, are working around the research of Daniel Muijs and David Reynolds on Effective Teacher Behaviours. The data collected come primarily from pupils' outcomes across four schools, but qualitative data are also collected through collaborative lesson observations. Once again, the lessons learnt are that when planning for CPD provision, the impact and evaluation of impact also has to be planned at the outset, and that external evaluation of CPD is also invaluable.

It cannot be denied that finding ways of measuring impact is a complicated and time-consuming process, but by now it should be obvious that a meaningful process of professional development cannot be based on quick fixes and magic bullets. It is also becoming clear that TSAs have a fundamental part to play in pushing an R&D agenda. Joint practice development, sharing of expertise and CPD, and data gathering across institutions are all very positive aspects of such alliances, led in great part through steering committees within the TSAs. In Cramlington's case, a bank of videos featuring an array of lessons or parts of lessons is being developed, one that all partners can access for deconstruction and discussion. The next step would be to pull resources together within the TSA to secure a researcher in residence, something that other TSAs are also considering.

Conclusion

There is ample evidence that schools are proactively seeking to make their communities more research-informed and research-engaged. The benefits are obvious. What we have learnt from the examples above is that links with other educational institutions are a fantastic way of ensuring that the work undertaken by teachers is more rigorous, and that expertise can be harnessed to fill in training gaps in terms of research methods. Conversely, universities are keen to collaborate with schools to ensure that the research they conduct is relevant, and is put to use. The emerging advice to schools, therefore, is to define their projects and contact their local universities, or approach other institutions such as the Centre for the Use of Research and Evidence in Education (CUREE).[8] Many partnerships are also currently fostered through the CfBT;[9] the work that they have done in supporting teacher-led action research is to be commended. Much of the work produced is also published, a great resource to ensure that research is cumulated and that new enquiries can build on existing ones.

Take-out messages:

- **TAKE-OUT ①:** Time must be found and created. Practitioner research must be prioritized as an essential part of professional development rather than becoming an additional burden.
- **TAKE-OUT ②:** To ensure teacher buy-in, supporting structures must be in place. The format is likely to be tweaked over the years, and it is important not to give up too easily. It is recommended to start with the evaluation in mind.
- **TAKE-OUT ③:** Coming up with a worthwhile enquiry is time consuming, but the time is well-invested. It will ensure rich professional dialogue leading to improved outcomes for students. Support must be offered at this early stage and input must be carefully thought through. Training in research methods should be on offer.
- **TAKE-OUT ④:** Starting points such as the EEF Teaching and Learning toolkit or the Sutton Report, as well as further reading, must be made available. Different levels of experience must be catered for. External expertise, perhaps in the form of research partners, is advisable.
- **TAKE-OUT ⑤:** Findings must be shared and carefully curated to ensure that evidence is cumulated and that teachers' work is celebrated.

Chapter appendix

The Evaluation Guidance Template provided to Park High teachers is set out in Table 7.1.

Table 7.1: Park High Evaluation Guidance Template

1	AIMS – WHAT IS YOUR ENQUIRY QUESTION? WHAT DO YOU WANT TO ACHIEVE?
	Who are your target pupils? What do you know about them? In which ways would you like to see them improve? Can you gather evidence to build a profile of these students?
2	PLANNING – WHAT APPROACHES WILL YOU TAKE?
	What is your planned approach? Which strategies will you implement in your planning? What further reading or research do you need to do, or need support with? Do you know of any colleagues who have already tried similar strategies with these students? Do you know colleagues from other schools who have tried something similar?

3	DELIVERY – WHAT WILL THE APPROACH LOOK LIKE IN THE LESSON AND IN YOUR PLANNING?
	What are your ideas so far to prompt the desired outcomes? What are the barriers? What is likely to go wrong and how will you plan for this?
4	METHODS – DESIGNING YOUR EVALUATION
	What qualitative and quantitative measures will you use to evaluate your approaches? What baselines and measures will you use to assess the impact of the intervention?
5	ONGOING REVIEW AND REFLECTION
	What went well and what outcomes were observed? What does your evidence tell you? What will you persevere with? What do you need to review and try next? Why do you think the approaches were successful/not successful?
6	IMPACT – SHARE YOUR RESULTS
	How will you share/present your results? How will you disseminate your findings? What do you think still needs to be researched further?

Further reading

Useful starting points for practitioner research:

1. **Education Endowment Foundation Teaching and Learning Toolkit** (regularly updated), available via the 'Teaching and Learning Toolkit' section of the EEF's website (http://educationendowmentfoundation. org.uk/toolkit)
2. **Education Endowment Foundation DIY Evaluation Guide** (regularly updated), available via the 'Evaluation' section of the EEF's website (http://educationendowmentfoundation.org.uk/evaluation)
3. **Sutton Trust Report (2014)** *What Makes Great Teaching? Review of the underpinning research*, available at: www.suttontrust.com/ researcharchive/great-teaching/
4. **BERA RSA Interim Report (2014)** *The Role of Research in Teacher Education: Reviewing the evidence*, available at: www.bera.ac.uk/wp-content/uploads/2014/02/BERA-RSA-Interim-Report.pdf
5. **BERA RSA Report (2014)** *Research and The Teaching Profession: Building capacity for a self-improving education system*, available at:

www.bera.ac.uk/wp-content/uploads/2013/12/BERA-RSA-Research-Teaching-Profession-FULL-REPORT-for-web.pdf

6. **Sutton Trust Report (2011)** *Improving the Impact of Teachers on Pupil Achievement in the UK,* **interim and final reports** both available at: www.suttontrust.com/

7. **The NFER Report (2012)** *What leads to positive change in teaching practice?*, available at: http://www.nfer.ac.uk/publications/rctl01/rctl01_home.cfm

8. **The Centre for the Use of Research Evidence in Education (CUREE)/ Pearson School Improvement Report (2012)** *Understanding What Enables High Quality Professional Learning: A report on the research evidence,* available at: http://www.curee.co.uk/files/publication/[site-timestamp]/CUREE-Report.pdf

9. *Sandringham School Learning Journal,* available at: www.sandagogy.co.uk/learning/?q=upload/sandringham-learning-journal.

Endnotes

[1] The Office for Standards in Education (Ofsted) is England's school inspection body.
[2] GCSEs are the standard academic qualifications taken by students aged 14–16 in secondary education in England, Wales, and Northern Ireland.
[3] AQA is a UK based examination board, see www.aqa.org.uk/.
[4] See http://tdtrust.org/nten/home/.
[5] See https://cramlingtonmuse.wordpress.com/cramlington-learning-villages-learning-and-teaching-bulletin/.
[6] See http://tdtrust.org/nten/home/.
[7] See www.gov.uk/the-national-research-and-development-network.
[8] See: www.curee.co.uk/.
[9] See: www.cfbt.com/.

References

The British Educational Research Association/The Royal Society for the Encouragement of Arts, Manufacturing and Commerce (2014) *The Role of Research in Teacher Education: Reviewing the evidence.* Online. www.bera.ac.uk/wp-content/uploads/2014/02/BERA-RSA-Interim-Report.pdf(accessed 8 November 2014).

The Sutton Trust (2011) *Improving the Impact of Teachers on Pupil Achievement in the UK.* Online. www.suttontrust.com/researcharchive/improving-impact-teachers-pupil-achievement-uk-interim-findings/ (accessed 8 November 2014).

Wiliam, D. (2010) *Teacher Quality: Why it matters, and how to get more of it.* Online. www.dylanwiliam.org/Dylan_Wiliams_website/Papers.html (accessed 8 November 2014).

— (2011) *How do we Prepare Students for a World we Cannot Imagine?* Online. www.newvisionsforeducation.org.uk/2011/12/06/how-do-we-prepare-students-for-a-world-we-cannot-imagine/ (accessed 8 November 2014).

Chapter 8

Impractical research: Overcoming the obstacles to becoming an evidence-informed school

Clare Roberts

Chapter overview

This chapter tells the story of a programme of action research conducted over the course of a year in a UK secondary school. Building on the author's evaluation of the programme, it highlights where the school leaders and teachers ran into difficulties and makes recommendations as to how these could have been avoided. In particular, two issues are highlighted that are vital to the successful facilitation of collaborative action research. The first is the headteachers' communication of their vision for action research and ongoing support for the programme, along with the provision of structures relating to incentives and accountability. The second relates to resources available to teachers engaging in action research, both in terms of the time available to them and in terms of their access to published research and expertise. The chapter concludes by suggesting that while action research is a powerful method of school improvement, it requires careful planning by senior leaders and a change of school culture if it is to be truly effective.

The move to whole-school action research

As part of the 'self-improving school system', schools in England need to find ways of providing staff with a diverse range of options for Continuing Professional Development (CPD). They must seek to cater for different phases of development and preferred learning styles. Fortunately, training done 'to' the whole teaching staff sat in a hall is fast becoming a thing of the past. Effective teacher training is now known to be collaborative, sustained over time, and self-directed, but also targeted to meet the school's needs, with teachers conceptualized as learners and the school as a learning community (Clarke and Hollingsworth, 2002; Cordingley and Bell, 2012).

Many schools are opting for one form of CPD that ticks all of these boxes: action research. Originating in the work of socio-psychologist Kurt Lewin, action research has long been employed by individual teachers as a means by which to instigate change. More recently, action research has found itself on the CPD 'menu' as a holistic and collaborative approach for teachers to self-direct specific improvements in their practice, feeding into School Improvement Plans.

A movement towards encouraging teacher research began after David Hargreaves's 1996 Teacher Training Agency annual lecture, in which he heavily criticized educational research for not being closely enough aligned with teaching and classrooms, the two existing as separate entities (Hargreaves, 1996). Several initiatives were born out of this criticism, some of which encouraged individuals to carry out research, for example the National Teacher Research Panel and the National College's Research Associate programme (Godfrey, 2014). Others sought to encourage schools themselves to become research institutions, for example the Forum for Learning and Research in Education (FLARE), which aimed to transform schools in Essex into research-rich institutions (Handscomb and MacBeath, 2003). Although there has been an increasing drive for schools to adopt this approach, a review of the literature suggests that little practical advice exists for school leaders who want to be successful at implementing action research as a form of CPD. Much of the literature assumes that practitioners will be working alone (as they traditionally have), rather than as part of a school-wide CPD programme, and gives step-by-step guides to carrying out research. Given that much CPD in the past has been led 'from the front', in specific time-slots in line with teacher 'directed time', and used to disseminate information as opposed to attempting to create it, it is vital that, in order to embrace wholescale action research, schools are well-equipped to bring about the necessary changes in the way they operate and conduct CPD.

Setting up the programme

My school is a small 11–16 comprehensive in an urban area with 'challenging' features common to inner-city schools, such as higher than national average proportions of English as an Additional Language (EAL), Free School Meals (FSM), and Special Educational Needs (SEN) students, and high staff turnover. It has a small teaching staff of 45 teachers. The Office for Standards in Education (Ofsted), England's school inspection body, had recently graded the school as 'good', on a scale where schools are 'inadequate', 'satisfactory', 'good', or 'outstanding'. As part of the school's attempt to move from 'good' to 'outstanding' in this ratings system, the senior leadership team decided to move towards a more self-directed model of CPD, wanting to give teachers greater responsibility and choice about the kinds of CPD in which they participated. Teachers were asked to select 20 hours from a 'menu' of CPD choices, including cross-curricular projects, action research, half-hour drop-in sessions run by current teaching staff, and group sessions with external consultants aimed at improving specific areas of practice. The 20 hours were linked to the school's appraisal system, in line with national expectations. As a result of the introduction of performance-related pay in schools from September 2014, CPD for the 2013/14 academic year was also explicitly linked to pay progression via appraisal. In order to pass their appraisals, teachers needed to provide evidence of these 20 hours of professional development. A third-year teacher, I was given responsibility for running the school's programme of action research, line-managed by the assistant headteacher with responsibility for CPD and teaching and learning.

In September 2013, I attended two sessions run by the Expansive Education Network (see *resource box 8.1*), aimed predominantly at schools wishing to encourage small groups of their teachers to engage in action research. The focus was on the steps required to formulate a research question, carry out research, and present evidence, as opposed to how action research can practically be carried out in a school. As a result of these sessions, I was able to design a programme of research for my school, aiming for two cycles of research, one to be completed with presentations given in January, and the other to be completed by July. My line manager and I agreed that a nine-hour allocation of CPD time was adequate for carrying out both research cycles. In October 2013, teaching staff were required to select their 20 hours of CPD options. I presented the action research programme to staff, and 12 teachers opted in to the programme. At a further session they selected partners to work with, and were asked to send back a document detailing their research question. None of the six pairs had difficulty identifying an appropriate area to focus on and all produced coherent action plans. Over the course of the year, two more whole-group meetings were held where pairs gave presentations on their findings to the rest of the group. I met each pair briefly on a monthly basis to check their progress and help with any issues.

> RESOURCE BOX 8.1:
>
> THE EXPANSIVE EDUCATION NETWORK:
> www.expansiveeducation.net/
> Championing the idea that education must fundamentally concern itself with expanding young people's capacity to deal with real-world complexity and uncertainty, the Expansive Education Network supports schools to engage in action research. Their website provides examples of completed action research projects and suggests possible resources that teachers can use in their projects.

Problems and solutions

From my observations throughout the year, and from interviews conducted with eight teacher participants, my line manager, and the headteacher at the end of the academic year, I was able to identify two general problem areas that arose while teachers were conducting research. Firstly, there were issues with the senior team's leadership of the programme, in particular the communication of vision, ongoing support for the programme, and the way the school incentivized and held its teachers to account. Secondly, there were issues with the resources available to teachers, both in terms of time available to them and in terms of their access to published research and expertise. I explore each of these below.

Leadership and vision

The headteacher and head of teaching and learning were very clear about why they had introduced the programme of action research. They knew all the benefits for students associated with teachers carrying out their own research, wanted to challenge teachers intellectually and encourage risk taking, and welcomed this kind of personalized, sustained, and collaborative approach. However, the teachers completing the programme did not share their vision. For example, discussions with teachers on the programme revealed perspectives such as:

> I knew what I was doing but not why I was doing it. We needed a clearer sharing and understanding of the vision, one which went deeper than just 'I'm doing this because it's my CPD' to one which was 'I'm doing this because I really want to improve and help others in the school improve as well.'

School leaders needed not only to set up the programme with good intentions about the outcomes, but also to ensure that teachers knew why action research was effective and how it fed into the school's wider vision for teaching and learning. Teachers also commented on a lack of engagement with the research programme by the senior leadership team (SLT), beyond initial warnings about not completing sufficient hours of CPD. For example:

> SLT needed to get behind it more and be enthusiastic that we were doing research for the school, mention it in briefings, invite us to share our findings, say thank you.

Senior leaders needed to ensure that the action research programme received good internal 'PR', whether this was by mentioning it in staff briefings, inviting more teachers to publicize their research internally, or even just by informally acknowledging it. Some teachers even expressed this in terms of accountability and appraisal – they wanted the senior leadership to hold them accountable for carrying out research, probably because this would have sent a stronger message that their research was important for the school's development. By not adequately acknowledging it, by focusing on the product and not on the process, school leaders missed crucial opportunities to signal to staff that their work was valuable and purposeful and, in doing so, potentially hindered the research. My first key lesson is that school leaders should formulate and communicate a clear vision for teacher research: they should carefully consider how they will make teachers feel their research is valued, and how they will continuously signal this and show their support throughout the year.

Incentives

Linked to this, there were also issues with the way school leaders incentivized teachers to carry out action research. In linking CPD to appraisal, the school was attempting to ensure that all teachers made a commitment to improving themselves as professionals. However, the negative framing of this incentive – 'complete twenty hours or fail your appraisal' – particularly when it was linked to pay progression, did not in fact create the *professional* attitude needed for action research. Recent national and local strikes, and multiple voices from within the teaching profession and outside it, have rallied against what they see as a climate of decreasing teacher autonomy and an erosion of teacher professionalism (Pedder *et al.*, 2010). The medical profession shares similar concerns, but this is a profession with research at its core (Goldacre, 2013). Doctors begin their careers expecting to make a contribution to medical research, and are trusted to do so as professionals

(Hargreaves, 1996). Teachers too need to be placed in a position of trust with regard to their research – specifying that they need to complete a certain number of hours works against the attitude and professionalism required for teacher enquiry. Most of the teachers at my school were very clear that they did not need this kind of incentive to carry out research, the majority saying that they were intrinsically motivated to carry it out by their desire to improve student outcomes and by the opportunity to collaborate. As one teacher said:

> I thought it was a good opportunity to work with a colleague. You rarely get the chance to collaborate and exchange ideas. It was good to both discuss areas we'd like to work on and then collaborate on ideas – I found that really good, that's why it appealed to me.

Another explained that she wanted to use action research as a method of extending her networks across the school, and another said that it felt good to have someone in the room 'not judging you'. One teacher explained the confidence boost and impetus to reflect that was brought about by collaborating with a colleague:

> You feel more confident working with someone else – when you're trying new things. It's good to reflect with someone as well. With normal CPD, you might implement it but there isn't that reflection.

Teachers also cited the desire simply to be in each other's classrooms, as they felt as though they otherwise lacked the opportunity to observe and learn from colleagues.

On the other hand, for a few teachers on the programme, the idea that they could 'tick off' nine hours of their CPD for their appraisal was the motivating factor for joining the programme. These teachers did not carry out meaningful research and their main goal became finding enough evidence that they had completed nine hours of CPD. It would be easy to say that these teachers were 'lazy', and when I brought up this issue with my line manager, it was suggested that some teachers innately lacked the ability to work proactively, which amounts to the same thing. However, I think that this ignores the issues being discussed in this chapter, which senior leaders should be aware of when thinking about introducing action research. The vast majority of teachers, given the right balance of support and encouragement, would probably derive a lot from the experience of completing action research. Encouragement needs to come in the form of trusting teachers as professionals, rather than in giving them minimum targets to be evidenced at an appraisal. Negative framing of incentives did not in fact achieve the desired outcome, which was to ensure that teachers carried out meaningful research, and it probably contributed to a sense of de-professionalism – treat teachers as tick-list machines and they will behave like this. Senior leaders need to bear in mind the nature of research, that it lies at the heart of professionalism, and they need to treat teachers like autonomous professionals if they want to get the best results from teacher research.

Time

In addition to issues of vision, leadership, and incentives, teachers had significant problems with finding the time to work together on research. For the action research programme at my school, in October 2013 teachers chose who they wanted to work with and then came up with a research question. They then compared timetables to see when it was possible to observe classes and meet each other. The structure of the timetable meant that all pairs had difficulties finding appropriate classes to work with. For example, one pair wanted to research Year 9 behaviour, but were both teaching Year 9 at the same time. All pairs had to modify their research questions, and in some pairs the structure of the school timetable prevented them from working together at all, as they had no times when one was free to observe the other. The school budget did not allow for the provision of cover, so some teachers asked others to cover their lessons and simply went in for a ten-minute slot to observe their partner. Despite this, the fact that teachers could not access each other was the single biggest difficulty of the programme.

School leaders looking to start up programmes of action research need to put serious thought into how they will practically ensure that teachers can work together. Either they need to be willing to budget for a number of hours of cover, or they need to plan in advance for CPD when they draw up the school timetable to ensure that teachers who wish to work together can do so. As organizationally difficult as this may seem, it would also go a long way to signal to teachers that the school is serious about supporting them with their research and about becoming a research-orientated community.

A related problem encountered by teachers was a difficulty in managing their time and prioritizing action research. One commented:

> We felt like we ran out of time. There's just so much to do and other things to do, so many other CPD and after school things

and intervention, it eats into your time. You kind of think you've got ages, and then time runs out.

Another teacher highlighted the effect of the unpredictable elements of a teacher's job and how these affected the research:

Realistically as a classroom teacher and form teacher, we're dealing with behaviour issues constantly. You just can't plan your time because that's the nature of schools, things just happen and you have to react pretty much immediately. And that's where it became difficult to complete the research.

Concerns around teacher workload are well-documented. In setting up a programme of action research, or indeed any CPD programme, it is vital that senior leaders ensure that teachers can manage their workload comfortably as well as doing their research. Disappointingly, many textbooks outlining how to do action research take the line that teachers will never have enough time for research, and that they should be prepared to make sacrifices of personal time in order to complete it. This seems to assume that schools will not make research enough of a priority to give teachers time to complete it. In hindsight, nine hours were inadequate for completing two cycles of research and I would question whether it is even possible to quantify the time a teacher will need to find an answer to a complex problem. Solutions to this will depend on the school. In my school, teachers actually requested to be given a weekly time slot when they had to come and talk about their research. It seems odd that teachers themselves would actually request to be micromanaged in this way, however they genuinely felt as though they needed to be forced to prioritize the time. Ideally, in order for teachers not to feel guilty about prioritizing research, a shift in the culture of the school is required so that research becomes the driving force for the school's improvement and is embedded in the culture. However, I suspect that there are many obstacles for senior leaders to navigate in bringing about this shift. Perhaps in the short term, leaders will have to resort to forced prioritization or other methods.

Access to research

As has been discussed in this book (for example, see Chapter 7), many teachers report difficulties in accessing literature about their chosen field of research, which would have made it easier for them to home in on possible solutions. Unless completing a master's degree or PhD at a higher education institution, teachers did not have access to journals and therefore struggled to come up with solutions beyond the scope of what was already known by teachers in their department or personal networks. This is certainly an issue senior leaders need to consider, as access to a research database is a key requirement for teachers carrying out professional research. Some teachers wanted more access to a 'specialist' in their field. For example, two teachers researching responding to marking with students with special educational needs found that they themselves could not solve the problems they had: they felt as though they needed to talk to somebody with the relevant expertise. Schools should make more use of their networks and links to other schools to facilitate access to this 'specialist expertise' in conjunction with action research. This is something else worth considering when senior leaders are designing programmes of action research.

Conclusion

Although these issues arose in the specific context of my school, I think they are certainly worth considering by any senior leaders wishing to implement action research at their schools. Perhaps more importantly, even facing these problems most teachers participating in the action research learnt a great deal and wanted to take part again. Action research is clearly a very powerful method of school improvement, but it needs careful planning by senior leaders and a change of school culture if it is to be truly effective.

Take-out messages

- **TAKE-OUT ①:** School leaders need to have a clear vision for their programme of action research and communicate this to participants and the wider school community.
- **TAKE-OUT ②:** School leaders need to lead and champion the programme throughout its duration, clearly integrating it into school improvement plans.
- **TAKE-OUT ③:** School leaders need to foster a culture of trust and professionalism in which teachers feel that they are making a meaningful contribution to the school's knowledge base.
- **TAKE-OUT ④:** School leaders need to plan the timetable so that teachers are able to work together effectively or provide cover if this is not possible.
- **TAKE-OUT ⑤:** School leaders need to create a research culture at school where teacher research has high support and is prioritized by staff.

- **TAKE-OUT ⑥**: School leaders need to find ways of facilitating access to journals and specialists, possibly by making better use of existing networks.

References

Clarke, D.J., and Hollingsworth, H. (2002) 'Elaborating a model of teacher professional growth'. *Teaching and Teacher Education*, 18 (8), 947–67.

Cordingley, P., and Bell, M. (2012) *Understanding What Enables High Quality Professional Learning: A report on the research evidence*. London: Centre for the Use of Research Evidence in Education and Pearson.

Godfrey, D. (2014) 'Leadership of schools as research-led organisations in the English educational environment: Cultivating a research engaged school culture'. *Educational Management Administration and Leadership*. Early online publication. http://ema.sagepub.com/content/early/2014/02/20/1741143213508294.full (accessed 19 January 2015; requires subscription).

Goldacre, B. (2013) *Building Evidence into Education*. London: Department for Education. Online. http://media.education.gov.uk/assets/files/pdf/b/ben%20goldacre%20paper.pdf (accessed 25 January 2015).

Handscomb, G., and MacBeath, J. (2003) *The Research-Engaged School*. Colchester: Essex County Council, Forum for Learning and Research Enquiry (FLARE).

Hargreaves, D. (1996) *The Teacher Training Agency Annual Lecture 1996: Teaching as Research-Based Profession: Possibilities and prospects*. Online. http://eppi.ioe.ac.uk/cms/Portals/0/PDF%20reviews%20and%20summaries/TTA%20Hargreaves%20lecture.pdf (accessed 14 January 2013).

Pedder, D., Opfer, V.D., McCormick, R., and Storey, A. (2010) '"Schools and Continuing Professional Development in England – State of the Nation" research study: Policy context, aims and design'. *Curriculum Journal*, 21 (4), 365–94.

Chapter 9

Teacher data use for improving teaching and learning
Jonathan Supovitz

Chapter overview

In this chapter I describe an intervention designed to facilitate teacher use of instructional and student performance data to improve teaching and learning outcomes. The chapter has three sections. First, I provide an overview of the *Linking intervention*, a US programme designed to provide Grades 1 to 5 (ages 6 to 11) mathematics teachers with regular, facilitated conversations about data on their instruction, examined in conjunction with data on the learning of their students. Second, I describe the results of the experimental study that assessed the intervention's impact. Third, I discuss the implications for school data use practices. Overall I suggest that the Linking study reveals several ways in which we can refine data experiences for teachers in order to better align the data and their purpose and better support improvements in the teaching and learning process.

Introduction

The data use movement has all the classic symptoms of a solution looking for a problem. Calls for practitioner 'data use' have spurred a wide variety of reforms all across the education system – data protocols for teachers and school leaders, data dashboard systems that collect and display an array of indicators, the formation of school data teams that conduct data-informed inquiries into groups of students, and specific formative assessment classroom techniques. From this abundance of approaches it is increasingly apparent that 'data use' means different things to decision-makers at different levels of the education system, and that the type and frequency of the data, mode of enquiry, and decision-making processes look quite different according to role, situation, and purpose (Supovitz, 2013; Marsh, 2012). Thus, when we talk about 'data use', we must ask 'for whom?' and 'for what purpose?'

This chapter focuses on what it means for teachers to productively use data on teaching and learning to enhance instructional and student outcomes. The recommendations it makes are derived from the findings of an experimental study that examined the effects of an intervention designed to help teachers connect data on their teaching with data on the learning of their students for the purpose of informing subsequent instruction that can lead to better student outcomes. The hypothesis of the study was that a particularly powerful use of data is to examine the connection between two data points – the instructional choices that teachers make and the learning outcomes of students. Thus, 'data use' in this study means facilitating teachers' analytical experiences of linking data on teaching to data on student learning.

Overview of the Linking intervention

The 'Linking Study' involved a research team from the Consortium for Policy Research in Education at the University of Pennsylvania in the United States working collaboratively with a regional school district to develop and study the impacts of an intervention that provided Grades 1 to 5 (ages 6 to 11) mathematics teachers with cyclical and facilitated conversations about data on their instruction, examined in conjunction with data on the learning of their students. The intervention was conducted within an experimental framework, with teachers in grade-level teams randomly assigned to participate in the experience or to continue with their usual practice of examining only student end-of-unit test data in their grade-level teams.

The Linking intervention consisted of providing a random sub-sample of teacher grade-level teams with written feedback on a videotaped lesson, followed by a facilitated discussion of both their teaching and their students' learning as represented on that unit's end-of-unit assessment. The facilitated discussions took place during the grade-level team meeting shortly after the unit was completed.

Treatment teachers received feedback from their lesson in two stages. First, they received private feedback by email within one week of the observed lesson, provided by a trained observer. The feedback was written in prose, rather than numerical ratings, and was written to balance both positive things about the lesson and areas for improvement, in accordance with the literature on effective performance feedback (Kluger and DeNisi, 1996). The feedback focused on the academic rigour of the lesson and the teachers' interactions with students (accountable talk). The feedback was sent via email to the teacher within one week of the observed lesson, regardless of when this took place in the timeline of the unit, so that the teacher received feedback as close to the lesson itself as possible. The observers also wrote feedback for each lesson of the control group teachers and provided it to them at the end of the study. The second component of feedback on the observed lesson came during a subsequent professional learning community (PLC) meeting. At the end of the mathematics unit, the teachers met in their professional learning community and followed a structured routine that was facilitated by a trained facilitator.

Each teacher brought their students' end-of-unit test data with them to the 45-minute treatment group grade-level team meeting.[1] Also, in advance of the meeting the facilitator chose one or two test items that were central to the focus of the unit and asked students to show their work. The design for the PLC meeting itself had two components. The first component, intended to take about 15 minutes, was to examine student test performance. Teachers were asked to group their students' work according to the strategy that students used to solve a problem, rather than by the correct answer. This allowed teachers to focus on students' solution strategies, which emphasizes how students are thinking about solving the mathematics problem and the efficiency of their solution strategies, rather than their ability to produce the correct answer. Facilitators were asked to guide the conversation using the following questions:

1. What different strategies do you see in your students' work on the test item?
2. In what way do these problem-solving strategies give you insight into how the students understand the big idea(s) of the unit?
3. Using this understanding, how can you support students to move towards more sophisticated strategies?

The second component of the PLC meeting was used to examine one or two selected video clips of a teacher's interaction with students so as to discuss examples of student–teacher interactions, or accountable talk. This component of the PLC session was intended to take about twenty minutes and facilitators were asked to guide this conversation using these questions:

1. How did the interaction begin?
2. What did the student(s) response(s) reveal about their understanding of the mathematics?
3. What was the teachers' follow-up?
4. Were there any missed opportunities? How might you have changed this interaction to learn even more?

At the end of this instructional conversation, participants were asked to spend the final ten minutes making connections between the instruction in the unit, as exemplified in the instructional discussion, and end-of-unit student test performance. Teachers in the control group were provided with a structured guide on how to examine student test data.

The intervention occurred in three cycles across three different mathematics units during the school year, which represented about a third of the units covered by teachers at their grade levels.

Impacts of the Linking intervention

The impacts of the Linking intervention were discovered by comparing the results of teachers in the treatment group with those in the comparison group on a variety of measures. First, the results of the experiment indicated moderate-sized effects – in the magnitude of about a third to a half standard deviations – on what teachers reported they learned about their teaching and their students' understanding when they responded to surveys. Second, and more objectively, there were statistical differences of the same magnitude between teachers in the treatment group and those in the control group on ratings of the quality of subsequent instructional practice, as measured by ratings of the videotaped lessons. For example, Figure 9.1 illustrates differences between treatment and control groups in relation to 'academic rigour', that is the rigour of the design and enactment of the lesson. These impacts on instructional practice were particularly notable because they were external judgements of instructional quality, rather than teacher self-report.

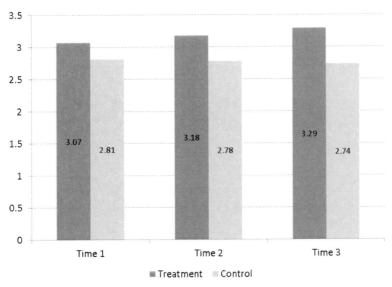

Figure 9.1: Differences in the adjusted means for treatment and control groups – 'academic rigour' outcomes

Third, there were small, but statistically significant, effects of the intervention on student learning over time, as measured by changes in student performance on the end-of-unit tests. Finally, and notably, teachers did not report being better prepared to use data, nor did they perceive a greater importance of data for their practice as a result of their experience. Thus, even though this intervention was about using data, it was not framed – nor was it perceived – as such. Rather, the intervention focused on examining teaching and learning, and the mechanism to do so was data on practice and performance.

Implications for school data-use practices

The design and impact of the Linking Study bring out a number of features of data interventions that can help school leaders and teachers use data to improve the quality of teaching and the learning of students. Here I highlight five key findings and discuss their implications for practice:

1) Use data to help teachers make connections between what they do – teaching – and what it produces – student learning. This is a more powerful approach than focusing on student test data alone.

A feature of the Linking intervention was that it connected what teachers do (teaching) with what it produces (student learning), and modelled for teachers ways to examine each of these aspects individually and to ask questions about the relationship between the two. A central premise of initiatives that bring data to teachers is that the data will provide some additional value that will inform their instructional choices, which will have a positive effect on student outcomes. Yet rarely, if ever, do we bring this process down to the classroom level to engage teachers in improvement of their craft and in gaining a deeper understanding of the relationship between their choices and the learning of their students. Systematic reflection about the choices we make, and their implications, is a central component of learning, yet we do not provide opportunities for teachers to make these connections in their practice.

2) Present data to teachers in a form that they naturally understand; do not make them learn research techniques in order to make sense of data.

What policymakers and researchers think of as 'data use' might need to be reframed so as to be more relevant for teachers. Many data interventions focus on giving teachers numerical test score information on their students. This creates two challenges for teachers. First, the numbers themselves contain relatively little information about how students understand the content, because they are mostly tallies of correct and incorrect responses. With little information to go on, teachers have little purchase on how to respond instructionally, and therefore are constrained to re-teaching and regrouping strategies (Supovitz, 2012). Second, providing teachers with numerical data requires that they have the quantitative analytical skills to manipulate the data to look for patterns. Few teachers are fluent in these skills that are the meat and potatoes of the world of researchers and policy analysts. In the Linking Study we tried to do things a little differently.

The data that teachers examined was presented in ways that were familiar to teachers: lesson feedback came in the form of written descriptions rather than ratings, and student data showed student work, not tabulations of test results. This helped teachers to focus on their instructional approaches and on the thinking processes of their students, rather than on acquiring new analytical skills to make sense of the data. The fact that the data were not presented to teachers in the form that we typically consider as 'data' may account for the survey findings that indicated that participants did not perceive that their skills in using data were improved, despite the fact that the evidence showed that their attention to the focus of the data examination – their instructional practices and student outcomes – did improve.

3) *Focus data collection, feedback, and conversations on high-leverage instructional activities, such as the rigour of lessons; the teacher–student and student–student interactions; and student problem-solving strategies represented in open-ended test items.*

A distinctive feature of the Linking Study was the emphasis on instructional practice data. It is surprisingly rare that teachers get to look at and discuss artefacts of their instructional practice. While there are initiatives like lesson studies (Lewis, 2002) that afford teachers the opportunity to debrief on the design and execution of lessons, these are not common in practice. When teachers do have opportunities to examine artefacts of their practice, the most frequent example is student test data, followed by lesson plans. As I have argued elsewhere (Supovitz, 2012), test results provide a limited window into instructional choices because they are often limited to recording whether students got the answer correct, and do not reflect the thinking process that produced the response. At the other end of the instructional production function, lesson plans show the intended design of a student's experience, but not the enacted practice. However, it should also be noted that the instructional intervention of this study was also its most unwieldy aspect. Arranging for videotapes of lessons and producing feedback from them was the most complicated and costly component of the study. Even so, this study raises significant questions about the importance of incorporating some measure of instruction into teachers' regular reflection opportunities.

The way that teachers were encouraged to examine student test data was another distinguishing aspect of the intervention. The analysis of student performance focused on distinguishing the strategies that students used to solve their problems and on characterizing these strategies along a learning progression of increased mastery of the content area within mathematics (i.e. addition, subtraction, multiplication, etc.). In this way, teachers were encouraged to consider how their students were thinking about the mathematics and move them towards more developmentally sophisticated solution strategies.

4) Make data-informed conversations an ongoing part of teachers' experiences, rather than isolated events.

An important feature of the Linking intervention was its cyclical nature. The treatment was designed to occur multiple times across the school year in mathematics areas that were repeated across the curriculum, so as to enhance teachers' opportunities to apply what they learned in one cycle to subsequent teaching in the next cycle. Theorists both within and outside of education have long hypothesized the importance of learning cycles to improvement (Deming, 1986; Smith and Ruff, 1998; Preskill and Torres, 1999). The curricular units that were the cycles of feedback had the benefit of being a natural learning unit, and of having an end-of-unit test for analysis. They were also part of the teachers' regular curriculum, as opposed to an externally derived interim assessment to capture student learning. While our capacity was constrained to three feedback cycles, which represented about a third of the mathematics units at a given grade, we might hypothesize that an even more regular and frequent feedback system would produce more powerful results.

5) Encourage safe discussion environments by putting up a firewall between data used to provide feedback for improvement and data used for accountability purposes.

Another component of the Linking intervention that deserves attention is the dynamic of reviewing data in grade-group meetings. These meetings were intended to leverage the multiple perspectives that participants brought to the process. Research on the examination of data in groups suggests some advantages of the collective, such as access to greater amounts of information (Hackman and Kaplan, 1974; Steiner, 1972), greater ability to detect errors in thinking (Hill, 1982; Shaw, 1981), and more perspectives for interpretation (Dennis, 1996). Yet, as the recruiting challenges in this study suggested, there may also be some reticence from teachers to expose their vulnerabilities to others in the current high-stakes environment. This is why we included survey questions about teachers' comfort with examining data in groups. The survey results indicated high levels of comfort with examining data in grade-group teams, but this may be a result of the subset of teachers who volunteered to participate in the study, and bears additional scrutiny in data interventions that ask teachers to expose their thinking in group settings.

Conclusion

The belief in data as a solution to problems in education at all levels of the system often produces ill-specified mismatches between the types and purposes of data and the problems they are intended to address. Too often we shoehorn misaligned, but readily available, data into a particular problem situation rather than looking for the right data to fit the problem. The Linking Study reveals several ways in which we can refine data experiences for teachers in order to better align the data and their purpose so as to better support improvements in the teaching and learning process.

Take-out messages

- **TAKE-OUT ①**: What helped make the Linking intervention effective was that we used data to help teachers make connections between what they do (instruction) and what this produces (student learning). Importantly, the intervention provided opportunities for teachers to examine each of these aspects individually and to ask questions about the relationship between the two.

- **TAKE-OUT ②**: There is a need to rethink how data are presented for teachers. If data are provided in a way that fails to help teachers understand student comprehension, then teachers will have limited insights as to how to instructionally respond. Data that help teachers focus reflectively on both their instructional approaches and the thinking processes of their students are most productive. To do this well, teachers also need opportunities to look at and discuss artefacts of their instructional practice, not just test results.

- **TAKE-OUT ③**: An important feature of the Linking intervention was its iterative, cyclical nature: teachers were engaged with the formative process repeatedly over the course of a school year. This builds on our understanding that regular and frequent feedback systems produce the most powerful results.

- **TAKE-OUT** ④: As is reflected elsewhere in this book (for example, Chapters 4 and 7), there is a positive dynamic of reviewing data in grade-group meetings. At the same time, there may also be some reticence from teachers to expose their vulnerabilities to others. To counter this requires the development of PLCs that facilitate safe discussion and risk-taking, and that are not linked to accountability.

Endnotes

[1] The curriculum contained end-of-unit assessments that included items where students were asked to explain their responses.

References

Deming, W.E. (1986) *Out of the Crisis*. Cambridge, MA: Massachusetts Institute of Technology Center for Advanced Engineering.

Dennis, A.R. (1996) 'Information exchange and use in small group decision making'. *Small Group Research*, 27 (4), 532–50.

Hackman, J.R., and Kaplan, R.E. (1974) 'Interventions into group process: An approach to improving the effectiveness of groups'. *Decision Sciences*, 5 (3), 459–80.

Hill, G.W. (1982) 'Group versus individual performance: Are N+1 heads better than one?' *Psychological Bulletin*, 91 (3), 517–39.

Kluger, A.N., and DeNisi, A. (1996) 'The effects of feedback interventions on performance: A historical review, a meta-analysis, and a preliminary feedback intervention theory'. *Psychological Bulletin*, 119 (2), 254–84.

Lewis, C.C. (2002) *Lesson Study: A handbook of teacher-led instructional change*. Philadelphia, PA: Research for Better Schools.

Marsh, J.A. (2012) 'Interventions promoting educators' use of data: Research insights and gaps'. *Teachers College Record*, 114 (11), 1–48.

Preskill, H., and Torres, R.T. (1999) *Evaluative Inquiry for Learning in Organizations*. Thousand Oaks, CA: Sage.

Sadler, D.R. (1989) 'Formative assessment and the design of instructional systems'. *Instructional Science*, 18 (2), 119–44.

Shaw, M. (1981) *Group Dynamics: The psychology of small group behavior*. 3rd ed. New York: McGraw-Hill.

Smith, D.R., and Ruff, D.J. (1998) 'Building a culture of inquiry: The School Quality Review Initiative'. In Allen, D (ed.) *Assessing Student Learning: From grading to understanding*. New York, NY: Teachers College Press, 164–82.

Steiner, I.D. (1972) *Group Process and Productivity*. New York: Academic Press.

Supovitz, J. (2012) 'Getting at student understanding: The key to teachers' use of test data'. *Teachers College Record*, 114, 1–29.

— (2013) 'Situated research design and methodological choices in formative program evaluation'. *National Society for the Study of Education Yearbook*, 112 (2), 372–99.

Chapter 10

Understanding impact and the cycle of enquiry

Carol Taylor and Karen Spence-Thomas

Chapter overview

At the London Centre for Leadership in Learning (LCLL), UCL Institute of Education (IOE), we have developed an approach to collaborative practitioner enquiry that supports schools in evidencing the difference that engaging in enquiry makes for staff professional learning and development and pupil learning and outcomes. In this chapter we set out the features of the methodology and its conceptual roots. We then describe how the approach has been applied by teaching school alliances (TSAs) involved in the National College Research Themes project between 2012 and 2014. From the 65 alliances involved, we draw out practical examples and case studies to illustrate how schools have been able to articulate, understand, and evidence change in staff practice and pupil learning with clarity and confidence. We conclude with a series of take-out messages for school leaders interested in applying this approach in practice.

Making a difference through collaborative enquiry

The white paper *The Importance of Teaching* (Department for Education, 2010) set out the UK government's plans to raise standards and improve the quality of teachers and school leadership through school-to-school support and peer-to-peer learning. With the aim of developing a 'self-improving system', England's national network of teaching schools have a key role to play in leading the training and professional development of teachers and headteachers. With this in mind, England's National College for Teaching and Leadership is supporting teaching schools to engage in action research centred on overarching national themes. In early 2012 the teaching schools research and development network[1] agreed the following three national themes as the focus of their research activities for 2012–14:

- **Theme 1:** What makes great pedagogy?
- **Theme 2:** What makes great professional development which leads to consistently great pedagogy?

- **Theme 3:** How can leaders lead successful teaching school alliances which enable the development of consistently great pedagogy?

The IOE, with its partners, Sheffield Hallam University (SHU), are working with a number of teaching schools to engage in collaborative enquiry with a view to producing robust evidence that will address the Theme 1 and Theme 2 questions. Specifically, our approach has been to:

- support teaching schools to engage in research and development activities
- provide opportunities for professional development, sharing expertise, and wider dissemination of 'what works'
- provide a forum for networking between teaching school leaders and teachers so that they can learn from each other.

Underpinning our approach has been the Connecting Professional Learning (C2L) framework, developed by Professor Alma Harris with Michelle Jones, which provides structure and direction for schools (Harris and Jones, 2012). The C2L framework draws on Harris and Jones's research about effective collaborative learning and their experience of supporting schools through professional learning communities (Harris and Jones, 2010). C2L places an emphasis on how to facilitate effective collaborative enquiry and proposes three interrelated phases of practitioner research: implementation, innovation, and impact (see Figure 10.1). IOE and SHU facilitators modelled the approach by convening termly regional enquiry clusters focusing on each phase in turn.

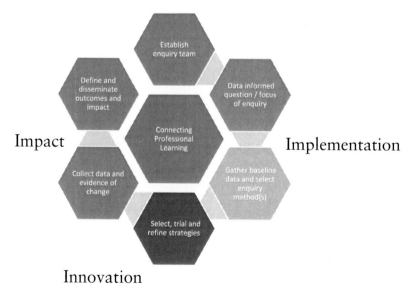

Figure 10.1: C2L Methodology

Our enquiry cycle included elements of an approach to evaluating impact developed at LCLL over a number of years. Earley and Porritt define impact as:

> ... the difference in staff behaviours, attitudes, skills and practice as a result of the professional development in which staff have engaged. Ultimately, impact is also the difference in the learning and experience of the children as a result of the change in staff practice and the latter becomes possible once there has been impact from [professional development].
>
> (Earley and Porritt, 2014: 121)

They argue that to evaluate impact effectively, staff need to be clear about the intended outcomes before the onset of the professional learning activity. Earley and Porritt also stress that time must be taken to gather evidence about current practice and pupil learning at the very beginning, in order that change can be captured throughout and can be confidently evaluated at the end of the project. If these twin aspects occur, it is more likely that practitioners will be able to understand and articulate the links between their own professional learning, changes in their practice, and the resultant impact on pupil learning and outcomes. Making these connections explicit means they can then begin to further embed those practices with increased confidence. The C2L methodology provides a common framework for tracking changes in professional learning, staff practices, and strategies trialled, against which the success of an entire project can be evaluated. A series of coaching and monitoring tools were also developed to prompt and support schools in capturing their baseline and final impact pictures in robust and rich ways using both qualitative and quantitative evidence.

Engaging with existing research

The overarching framework for the project also included two literature reviews – one each for Theme 1 (Husbands and Pearce, 2012) and Theme 2 (Stoll *et al.*, 2012): see Figures 10.2 and 10.3 respectively. Each review proposed nine claims that sought to bring together 'what is known' about great pedagogy and great professional development. Schools were encouraged to engage with these claims in a variety of creative ways in order to determine and refine their areas of focus and establish their starting points. The claims provided a firm and constant structure against which interim and summative findings have been brought together and analysed (Nelson *et al.*, 2014).

Theme 1: What makes great pedagogy? Nine strong claims from research

1. Effective pedagogies give serious consideration to pupil voice.

2. Effective pedagogies depend on behaviour (what teachers do), knowledge and understanding (what teachers know), and belief (why teachers act as they do).

3. Effective pedagogies involve thinking about longer term learning outcomes as well as short-term goals.

4. Effective pedagogies build on pupils' prior learning and experience.

5. Effective pedagogies involve scaffolding pupil learning.

6. Effective pedagogies draw on a range of techniques, including whole class, structured group work, guided learning, and individual activity.

7. Effective pedagogies focus on developing higher order thinking and meta-cognition, and make good use of dialogue and questioning in order to do so.

8. Effective pedagogies embed assessment for learning.

9. Effective pedagogies are inclusive and take the diverse needs of a range of learners, as well as matters of student equity, into account.

Figure 10.2: What makes great pedagogy?

(Husbands and Pearce, 2012)

Schools engaged in Theme 1 commonly explored shared pedagogical issues of interest, for example those related to mathematics, literacy, or writing. Others, meanwhile, looked specifically at the transition between primary and secondary, or between Key Stage 4 and post-16. A number focused on more general aspects of pedagogy, including: independent learning; engagement; motivation; growth mindsets; and peer and teacher assessment. In almost every case the focus for the enquiry combined an aspect of the formal research base with a perceived need or development priority, perhaps identified by Ofsted (England's school inspectorate) or through internal evaluation.

Theme 2: What makes great CPD that leads to consistently great pedagogy?
Nine strong claims from research

---

1. Effective professional development starts with the end in mind.

2. Effective professional development challenges thinking as part of changing practice.

3. Effective professional development is based on assessment of individual and school needs.

4. Effective professional development involves connecting work-based learning and external expertise.

5. Effective professional learning opportunities are varied, rich, and sustainable.

6. Effective professional development uses action research and enquiry as key tools.

7. Effective professional development is strongly enhanced through collaborative learning and joint practice development.

8. Effective professional development is enhanced by creating professional learning communities within and between schools.

9. Effective professional development requires leadership to create the necessary conditions.

Figure 10.3: What makes great CPD that leads to consistently great pedagogy?

(Stoll *et al.*, 2012)

Schools and alliances working with Theme 2 exploited the cross-school dimension of their activity and chose to explore aspects of collaborative professional development, investigating whether, how, and in what ways working together with colleagues brings about change in staff and pupil learning. A significant number of research questions were therefore located around claims 6, 7, and 8. A range of collaborative approaches have been considered, including learning triads, action learning sets, coaching and mentoring, and practitioner enquiry itself, with a significant proportion of alliances looking closely at lesson study. In terms of a pedagogical focus for the professional development strategy, regularly occurring focuses include assessment for learning, effective questioning, developing cross-curricula literacy strategies, encouraging dialogic teaching, and mathematics strategies.

How to evidence change in staff learning and practice

Teaching school alliances explored a variety of ways of evaluating the impact of their work on staff knowledge and practices depending on their specific focuses. In keeping with the methodology, several developed a rich baseline picture relating to staff attitudes and practices in order to be able to show impact in relation to this. Many used questionnaires at the beginning and at later points in the enquiry process to assess changes in teacher beliefs, attitudes, skills, and knowledge. Classroom observations, interviews, and questionnaires added to the picture for some, as did feedback from school leaders and colleagues.

Lesson plans and resources, together with lesson observations, including video evidence, were also used, both as part of the professional development (PD) process itself and as a way of identifying changes in teacher practices and impact on learning. 'Softer' evidence, such as teacher self-perceptions, were collected and leaders were on occasions asked for their perceptions of change in their colleagues. In order to provide deeper insights into developments in teachers' behaviours and beliefs, learning journals, case studies, and evaluations of classroom change were also collected as evidence.

Throughout the project, participants were challenged to think about the collaborative nature of their work and, specifically, how professional relationships and dialogue bring about pedagogical change. Teachers became engaged in discussions about relational trust, the quality and level of talk in social networks, and the importance of learning conversations. These discussions also explored the nature of the evidence being gathered about changes in practice and learning and highlighted the challenges of mapping or monitoring the quality of professional dialogue over time. Examples of how schools did this are set out in *resource box 10.1* and *resource box 10.2*.

> RESOURCE BOX 10.1:
>
> **Leicester TSA (Rushey Mead)** –The five schools involved in this project each had their own enquiry focus, although all agreed on wanting to use the experience of introducing lesson study to change the culture of PD in their schools. Both baseline and impact evidence was collected from teacher and leader questionnaires, which allowed for open responses to many of the questions. These indicated an

overall positive shift in attitudes in relation to the value of this enquiry approach. The 'revelatory' opportunity that lesson study offers teachers to focus on the learning of particular pupils was identified as highly significant in challenging thinking. For example, staff reported:

> a raised understanding of the difference between what teachers think students understand and what they actually do understand.

Other illustrative quotations from questionnaires indicate the changes in pedagogy made following such insights. For instance, the process provided:

> an invaluable opportunity to be able to really just observe actions of targeted pupils that I perhaps hadn't noticed before. It was far easier to identify strategies that worked for those pupils in this manner than when you are focusing on a whole group.

There was also an insight into:

> how much assessment the class teacher can miss: how to organize the classroom better to cater for individuals.

RESOURCE BOX 10.2:

Cramlington TSA – The initial research question for this enquiry was 'what are appropriate professional development activities to support newly qualified teachers (NQTs) to develop effective teacher behaviours?' The project group began by 'visioning' where they wanted new teachers (and learners in their care) to be at the end of their NQT year. This resulted in a development programme focused on four teacher behaviours:

- classroom management
- classroom climate
- interactive teaching
- learning style.

Baseline evidence drew on an analysis of pupil performance for those taught by NQTs in previous years in all four participating schools. A common classroom observation pro forma was developed so that tracking the development of desired behaviours was consistent

131

across schools. Consistency was further enhanced through collaborative development events and mentor networking. Impact data were collected every term on pupil progress, with residuals assigned to each student based on their actual grade and their target grade and an average residual calculated for students and classes in the care of the NQTs. This was compared with parallel data from the previous year's NQTs. A positive impact was noted on both the effectiveness of teaching and on pupil learning compared with the previous cohort of NQTs.

Having the 'end in mind' at the outset supported a clear structure for the development programme and its evaluation. Schools also agreed that a shared language to describe effective teacher behaviours was one of the most effective strategies used in the enquiry. Perspectives on the success of the approach and its impact are nicely summarized in the following comment from a teacher working on a project to develop a toolkit to support teachers in their journey to outstanding teaching; in combination with observations and coaching:

> having to explain what, how and why you do something really forces you to truly look at your own practice and be honest with how successful it has been and re-look at mistakes you have made along the way ... this is a long term, no quick fix approach but one that is proving vital to personal development with our practice and maximizing impact with learners.

How to evidence change in pupil learning and outcomes

Husbands and Pearce introduce their summary of research literature with the critical link between good teaching and good learning, focusing attention on:

> ... what constitutes effective teaching, or, put differently, on the behaviours and action of good teachers: what it is that good teachers do to promote good learning.
>
> (Husbands and Pearce, 2012: 2)

We have already alluded to the challenges teachers face in better understanding precisely which changes or improvements in their practices make the critical difference for pupils and their learning. Of course, one way of identifying good learning is through the attainment of pupils in tests and formal assessments, and these were used by many partnerships to evaluate the success of their projects. As well as using pupil progress measures based on the national assessment framework, schools used internal assessments to gauge the understanding, skills, and knowledge of pupils before and after pedagogic interventions, to judge the effectiveness of introducing new pedagogies. Several schools acknowledge that attempts to correlate an intervention with an improvement in test outcomes needs to be treated with caution, most obviously because partnerships were usually comparing the progress of different cohorts of pupils. Where possible, these schools drew on further data such as pupil questionnaires, pupil work, lesson observations, and feedback from teachers and parents to at least triangulate or substantiate such claims.

A number of projects focused on pedagogies to improve pupil learning relied less on test performance; as did those seeking to improve independent learning skills, metacognition, engagement, or motivation. These enquiries tended to draw on pupil work scrutiny and student voice for their evidence base. Where changes in pedagogy were found to be successful, they were embedded into school practice in the participating schools and disseminated more widely, both within the teaching school alliances and through local authority, regional, and national events. The range and rigour of the evidence gathered enabled teachers to share the difference that their changed practice made to outcomes for their pupils with greater confidence and conviction. Examples of how schools did this are set out in *resource boxes 10.3 to 10.6*.

Resource box 10.3:

Herts and Bucks TSA – In this project, pupils were asked to select a topic and activity for a lesson starter, which they delivered to their peers. Baseline data from student surveys showed that although two-thirds of pupils had never been asked to take on responsibility for teaching part of a lesson, those who had done so 'overwhelmingly stated that it had helped them enjoy the lesson more and helped them learn more'.

Impact data, collected through a further student survey and through staff feedback, showed that the majority of pupils enjoyed choosing the topic and delivering part of the lesson and felt it helped both them and their peers learn. Teachers confirmed this, adding that it was particularly beneficial for those leading the activities, but that there was a need to provide greater guidance to some pupils.

RESOURCE BOX **10.4**:

Stourport TSA – The design of a 'thinking steps' model to improve mathematical problem solving was informed extensively by pupil voice, using feedback on what able problem solvers find useful. The model was:

> originally developed through listening to what pupils said were the most effective strategies for problem solving. At each stage of the research, we have developed the model in the light of feedback from the students.

Testing the ability to solve similar sets of problems before and after being taught the 'thinking steps' showed an increase of more than 30 per cent in scores. Following the initial trial, further improvements have been suggested.

RESOURCE BOX **10.5**:

Westdene TSA – This transition project addressed teachers' beliefs and expectations about what pupils could achieve in mathematics. Baseline data from surveys and interviews showed that teachers underestimated the prior knowledge and capability of pupils entering secondary school. As part of their approach, Year 6 and Year 7 teachers observed one another, lesson plans and materials were shared and a new approach to data transfer was introduced in which pupils were much more involved. Impact data showed that teachers' expectations had been raised and so had the progress of their pupils. By the end of the project, 93 per cent of Year 7 pupils were at or above target compared with 73 per cent in the Year 9 cohort who had not been part of the new approaches to transition.

RESOURCE BOX **10.6**:

Bishop Challoner TSA – After seven months of a project designed to improve progress in literacy, pupil data showed that, although overall progress of targeted pupils was slightly in advance of national expectations, there were groups of pupils who were progressing more rapidly than others. An attitudinal survey was used to gain insight into the preferred learning approaches of all pupils, and revealed a clear difference between the groups with different rates of progress.

The pedagogy was amended in the light of these interim findings. At the end of the project, 81 per cent of the targeted group met or exceeded national expectations of progress when judged against progress rates of comparable students in previous years (the national figure for three levels of progress was 69 per cent).

Take-out messages

- **TAKE-OUT** ①: Helping practitioners to connect their practice with what is already known about an issue of interest to them results in powerful professional learning.
- **TAKE-OUT** ②: Our approach requires staff to dig deeply into their practice and make connections between how they teach and how pupils learn.
- **TAKE-OUT** ③: Enabling teachers to centre an enquiry on the difference they wish to make for their pupils in their classrooms is highly motivating and excellent professional development.
- **TAKE-OUT** ④: Great professional development begins 'with the end in mind'. The approach supports staff to vision the hoped-for outcome of their work both in terms of their professional practice and in terms of pupil learning.
- **TAKE-OUT** ⑤: Great professional development also requires staff to be very clear about their starting points – the point of departure. What data need to be gathered at the baseline to evaluate impact?
- **TAKE-OUT** ⑥: Evidencing impact needs to be manageable for staff.
- **TAKE-OUT** ⑦: Schools are awash with data. Teachers and leaders need to be able to differentiate between how data are used for accountability purposes and how they can be interrogated to explore how pupils learn.

Endnotes

[1] See www.gov.uk/the-national-research-and-development-network.

References

Department for Education (2010) '*The Importance of Teaching: The schools white paper 2010*'. Online. www.education.gov.uk/schools/toolsandinitiatives/schoolswhitepaper/b0068570/the-importance-of-teaching (accessed 13 August 2013).

Earley, P., and Porritt, V. (2014) 'Evaluating the impact of professional development: The need for a student-focused approach'. *Professional Development in Education*, 40 (1), 112–29.

Harris, A., and Jones, M. (2010) *Professional Learning Communities in Action*. London: Leannta Press.

— (2012) *Connecting Professional Learning: Leading effective collaborative enquiry across teaching school alliances*. Nottingham: National College for School Leadership.

Husbands, C., and Pearce, J. (2012) *What Makes Great Pedagogy? Nine claims from research*. Nottingham: National College for School Leadership.

Nelson, R., Spence-Thomas, K., and Taylor, C. (2014) *National Research Themes Project: Final report*. Nottingham: National College for School Leadership.

Stoll, L., Harris, A., and Handscomb, G. (2012) *Great Professional Development which Leads to Consistently Great Pedagogy: Nine claims from research*. Nottingham: National College for School Leadership.

Chapter 11

Leveraging social networks for educational improvement

Kara S. Finnigan,[1] *Alan J. Daly,*
Nadine D. Hylton, and Jing Che

Chapter overview

This exploratory mixed-methods case study draws upon social network analyses, survey data, and interview data to examine the ways in which educators in low-performing schools and their central offices define, acquire, use, and share research-based evidence for school improvement. We discuss how network 'structure' and 'ties' affect the acquisition, proliferation, and use of research-based evidence. We bring to the forefront educators' understanding of research and other types of evidence, and shed light on how network structures in the district and in schools promote and constrict the flow and utilization of evidence.

Policy context

Spurred on by the passage of the No Child Left Behind Act (NCLB), school- and district-level reforms have targeted the elimination of the persistent achievement gap in US public schools. Embedded in the legislation is language encouraging educators and policymakers to align the acquisition and use of federal dollars with the use of research-based evidence, or 'scientifically based research'. Despite the overt push towards research-based evidence, there is limited empirical research on the use of, access to, and flow of research evidence in schools and districts (Honig and Coburn, 2008).

Under NCLB, schools and districts in the US must meet accountability mandates as measured by Adequate Yearly Progress (AYP) towards benchmarks. Failure to meet AYP results in a school or district being designated as 'in need of improvement' (INI), a status that is accompanied by progressive sanctions. According to the Department of Education, over 10,000 schools (eddataexpress.ed.gov) received INI designation for the academic year 2011/12, with many of these schools remaining in this provisional status rather than exiting sanctions.

Improving underperforming schools is a complex and multifaceted process. As such, school improvement must be conceptualized within a broader context, moving from examining the school as a singular unit for change to exploring the role of connections between schools and central offices in engendering change (Hightower *et al.*, 2002; Honig, 2006; Honig and Coburn, 2008; Hubbard *et al.*, 2006; Togneri and Anderson, 2003). In this exploratory study, we try to better understand why there may be limited progress under sanctions by using social network analyses to examine how low-performing schools and their central offices define, acquire, and use research-based evidence. We pay close attention to the relationships between central offices and schools as they relate to the flow of different types of evidence throughout a school system, and to the use of evidence in engendering change.

Research evidence, organizational learning, and social networks

Reform and learning are complex acts, and educators use a plethora of methods and techniques to make sense of multiple variables and contextual factors in an attempt to derive 'one right approach'. Similarly, the 'evidence' that educators utilize may be equally varied, from anecdotal evidence to personal experience and articles in the popular press. The lack of conceptual and practical clarity on how evidence is conceptualized, acquired, and used for innovation by educators at various levels in schools and districts (Argyris, 1999; Argyris and Schön, 1996; Huber, 1991; Levitt and March, 1988; March, 1991) is a primary catalyst for this study.

Barriers to the use of evidence, particularly research evidence, in schools and districts include the ambiguity of research material and the lack of applicability and relevance to daily practice (Massell and Goertz, 1999; Nelson, 1989). Furthermore, the lack of sustained opportunities to connect or link researchers and research consumers (educators) inhibits research evidence use (Nelson, 1989). External and internal relationships can also influence access to research evidence in an organization. External ties may permit new ideas or approaches grounded in research to enter the school or district through connections with external organizations, while internal ties provide greater access to expertise within the school or district (Honig and Coburn, 2008).

Social network theory provides an important framework and useful set of methods to understand whether educators have access to research-based evidence and whether underlying networks, both within a school and across a district, support or constrain efforts to bring about the necessary improvements to allow the school to exit accountability policy sanctions. A basic premise of social network theory is the concept of social capital, or 'the resources embedded in social relations and social structure which can be mobilized' (Lin, 2001: 24). The quality of these ties between individuals in a social system creates a structure that determines opportunities for social capital transactions and access to resources, information, and knowledge (Granovetter, 1973, 1982; Lin, 2001; Putnam, 1993, 1995). Prior research suggests that the network of ties within a system can either support or hinder organizational change (Krackhardt, 2001; Mohrman *et al.*, 2003; Tenkasi and Chesmore, 2003). As we show here, social network analysis (SNA) can reveal the underlying network structures and provide insights into the ways in which relationships facilitate the movement of evidence throughout a system.

Methods

Our exploratory case study (Yin, 2003) involves a mid-sized urban district with 34,000 students; 88 per cent of students are non-white, including 65 per cent African American students, 21 per cent Hispanic students, and 2 per cent students belonging to other minority groups. Additionally, 88 per cent of students are eligible for free or reduced price lunches. A mixed-methods approach was employed to collect interview and survey data between 2009 and 2011.

Survey data collection and analysis

Quantitative data included surveys of school and district leaders (n=113) and educators in three high schools (n=173). For the SNA questions we asked respondents to assess their relationships in various areas with school and district leaders or school staff on a 5-point interaction scale ranging from 1 (no interaction) to 5 (interactions 1–2 times a week). We also enquired about the individuals who brought research into the organization and mapped their centrality in relation to other actors (RE questions). We used a *bounded* approach for the school and district SNA surveys, which provided a more complete picture of the network and thus more valid results (Scott, 2000). Organizational learning (OL) questions were also included in the survey instrument. The final instrument was externally validated by researchers with expertise in this area and by practitioners, and tested in three schools. School and district SNA/RE/OL surveys administered online had response rates above 80 per cent.

Using UCINET software a series of network measures were calculated (Borgatti *et al.*, 2002). We focused on centrality measures to examine the acquisition and diffusion of research evidence, as highly central actors in a network have increased access to resources and the potential to create new linkages (Stuart, 1998; Tsai, 2000). Descriptive analyses of the RE and OL survey data were conducted using SPSS, as well as analysis of the RE items in combination with the SNA questions to consider the diffusion of research and other types of evidence schoolwide and districtwide.

Interview data

A semi-structured interview guide was used (Patton, 1990; Spradley, 1980) to interview 54 educators in three high schools. Interviews were audio-recorded and transcribed verbatim. We used inductive analyses to allow important themes to emerge out of the data (Patton, 1990), as well as a constant comparative analysis method (Boeije, 2002) through checking and rechecking emerging themes relating to evidence acquisition and use (Miles and Huberman, 1994). NVIVO software was used to assist in the coding and sorting of data.

Findings

Our findings across all data sources suggest that school staff primarily consulted data (not research) as 'research evidence' to make decisions, but used these data in superficial ways. Educators relied heavily on principals for evidence, but rarely connected with each other. Furthermore, we found sparse connections between central office leaders and school leaders. We discuss first the definition and acquisition of evidence in these schools, and then the use of evidence.

Definition and acquisition of evidence

To gain a better understanding of educators' definition of evidence and whether this involves research, we asked school staff to share their views of what they considered to be evidence. Our qualitative data suggest that staff had a narrow view of evidence, almost exclusively focusing on test scores or other administrative records and outcome data, with few interviewees mentioning practice-oriented or experiential evidence. In fact, several individuals equated 'evidence' and 'research evidence' with standardized test scores.

The term 'research' was occasionally used to refer to what other schools and districts were doing as part of their improvement efforts. However, several interviewees mentioned that although studies exist that show success in school improvement, they felt that their own context was unique, and that this research was not applicable to their context and could not inform their work. We also found that educators in schools were most likely to consult student performance data, followed by internal evaluations and district administrators, suggesting a more 'local,' context-specific approach to evidence for decision making.

Our interview data also found a degree of scepticism about different types of evidence. Some aspects of this distrust seemed related to a possible lack of knowledge as to how to interpret the data or research that was available. In addition, teachers raised concerns that many types of evidence were not at all useful for practice or improvement. Adding to this distrust, the staff also gave examples of data manipulation by central office staff as well as the broader education community. Although central office staff were considered central players in brokering access to certain types of evidence, for example data relating to student outcomes (as discussed in more detail below), the network structures inhibited the diffusion of these resources.

Many teachers also mentioned that their principals were a critical link to research, responsible for bringing different types of evidence into more formal discussions and sharing practices that were used in other classrooms. This was supported by our network data in two of the three schools. However, research evidence acquisition was also constrained by the principal. Thus, while we see the principal as a critical link in developing coherence around an approach, he or she may also serve as gatekeeper of this evidence, inhibiting access to additional sources or impeding schoolwide diffusion.

We also considered research use and diffusion across the district. Our survey of school and central office leaders indicates that 62 per cent of district leaders agreed or strongly agreed that time was made available to discuss research. However, the likelihood that these research-based ideas and practices diffused to school-level staff appears unlikely, given limited connectivity between central office leaders and principals. Network data related to who brings ideas from research into the district supports these findings, indicating that district staff are more central in terms of both outdegree and indegree. That is, they are more central in both getting ideas (t = 3.727, df = 92, p < .001) and sharing ideas (t = 2.076, df = 59, p < .05) from research, compared with site administrators.

Use of evidence

Educators in these low-performing schools report that they are most likely to discuss data informally (84 per cent). Additionally, they report discussing both research and data during formal meetings (67 per cent and 73 per cent respectively) and using both research and data to inform schoolwide decisions (76 per cent and 77 per cent respectively). However, as mentioned above, we found a narrow view of what counted as evidence, which may have inhibited the search for evidence that could have been more useful for identifying problems and solutions.

We also considered whether central actors in the networks were more likely to consult certain types of data, serving as 'opinion leaders' that activate peer networks (Rogers, 1995) and diffuse innovation to others. Our data indicate that central individuals in the emotional support network were less likely to consult the types and sources of evidence that were considered least credible, such as staff at another school, the popular press, and local experts. However, these findings did not hold for central figures in the expertise network, suggesting that when people seek out expertise they are likely to be connecting with individuals who are less selective in their use of evidence.

While our research is exploratory, it supports prior research in terms of a few key barriers to research acquisition and use. We found that barriers to evidence use included pressures to determine improvement strategies based upon monetary resources that were available (or not), and limited access to 'useable' evidence, meaning evidence that could clearly inform decisions, not just identify problem areas. We found that other types of evidence were more highly valued than research. In fact, 60 per cent of school staff believed that practitioner experience was more valuable than data; 48 per cent relied on strategies they knew to be effective without searching for evidence to support them; 27 per cent viewed research as not relevant; and 20 per cent thought a 'hunch' was better than evidence. This devaluing of evidence, including research-based evidence, is an important area that deserves further attention given the current push for greater attention to evidence-based decision making in schools and districts.

Take-out messages

This exploratory case study uncovered many themes that are relevant to districts and schools that are under pressure to improve. Below we outline our key themes and take-out messages:

- **TAKE-OUT ①:** Narrow definitions limit research acquisition and use. While educators appear to value access to a wide variety of evidence, the volume of evidence can be overwhelming, creating a 'data rich, information poor' environment that leads to little consideration of the credibility of evidence or even the relevance of different types of evidence.

- **TAKE-OUT ②:** Lack of diffusion of evidence both within schools and districtwide. We found that the underlying network structure relating to research evidence involved a central individual with relatively sparse ties between and among other network members. Moreover, the lack of connections between central office leaders and principals constrains the flow of evidence districtwide, particularly into these low-performing schools that are likely to need new ideas and practices to improve.
- **TAKE-OUT ③:** Weak affective connections. The difficulty of bringing about complex change in low-performing schools is compounded by the fact that affective or emotional relationships between administrators are extremely sparse, particularly those relating to vertical ties between central office and sites. Trust and reciprocal relationships are just as critical as instrumental or work-related ties if complex change is required.
- **TAKE-OUT ④:** Instrumental, yet superficial, use of evidence. Educators used research evidence in instrumental yet superficial ways, primarily to frame a solution to an existing problem without carefully analysing the problem. Staff had limited interactions with data, resulting in a limited understanding of how to interpret and utilize data in decision making.
- **TAKE-OUT ⑤:** Need for educators to be active generators of knowledge. New approaches to learning in schools and districts move the teacher from technician and implementer of 'research-based evidence', to active generator of knowledge and evidence that can be used to improve school-level outcomes. Of course, school staff must have the capacity to thoughtfully and rigorously engage with the process of gathering evidence, and apply it in a manner that goes beyond superficial use. Recent work in design-based research holds promise in this regard (Penuel *et al.*, 2011). Approaching the acquisition of evidence through research-based partnerships may be the key to sustainable change in low-performing schools and districts.

Endnotes
[1] The first two authors contributed equally to this chapter.

References
Argyris, C. (1999) *On Organizational Learning*. 2nd ed. Oxford: Blackwell.

Argyris, C., and Schön, D.A. (1996) *Organizational Learning II: Theory, method, and practice*. Reading, MA: Addison-Wesley.

Boeije, H. (2002) 'A purposeful approach to the constant comparative method in the analysis of qualitative interviews'. *Quality and Quantity*, 36 (4), 391–409.

Borgatti, S.P., Everett, M.G., and Freeman, L.C. (2002) UCINET for Windows: Software for social network analysis. Harvard, MA: Analytic Technologies.

Granovetter, M.S. (1973) 'The strength of weak ties'. *American Journal of Sociology*, 78 (6), 1,360–80.

— (1982) 'The strength of weak ties: A network theory revisited'. In Marsden, P.V., and Lin, N. (eds) *Social Structure and Network Analysis*. Beverly Hills, CA: Sage, 105–30.

Hightower, A.M., Knapp, M.S., Marsh, J.A., and McLaughlin, M.W. (eds) (2002) *School Districts and Instructional Renewal*. New York, NY: Teachers College Press.

Honig, M.I. (2006) 'Street-level bureaucracy revisited: Frontline district central-office administrators as boundary spanners in education policy implementation'. *Educational Evaluation and Policy Analysis*, 28 (4), 357–83.

Honig. M.I., and Coburn, C. (2008) 'Evidence-based decision making in school district central offices: Toward a policy research agenda'. *Educational Policy*, 22 (4), 578–608.

Hubbard, L., Mehan, H., and Stein, M.K. (2006) *Reform as Learning: School reform, organizational culture, and community politics in San Diego*. New York, NY: Routledge.

Huber, G.P. (1991) 'Organizational learning: The contributing processes and the literatures'. *Organization Science*, 2 (1), 88–115.

Krackhardt, D. (2001) 'Network conditions of organizational change'. Paper presented at the Academy of Management Annual Meeting, Washington, DC.

Levitt, B., and March, J.G. (1988) 'Organizational learning'. *Annual Review of Sociology*, 14, 319–40.

Lin, N. (2001) *Social Capital: A theory of social structure and* action. New York, NY: Cambridge University Press.

March, J.G. (1991) 'Exploration and exploitation in organizational learning'. *Organization Science*, 2 (1), 71–87.

Massell, D., and Goertz, M. (1999) 'Local strategies for building capacity: The district role in supporting instructional reform'. Paper presented at the Annual Meeting of the American Educational Research Association, Montreal, Canada, April.

Miles, M.B., and Huberman, A.M. (1994) *Qualitative Data Analysis*. 2nd ed. Thousand Oaks, CA: Sage.

Mohrman, S.A., Tenkasi, R.V., and Mohrman, A.M. (2003) 'The role of networks in fundamental organizational change: A grounded analysis'. *Journal of Applied Behavioral Science*, 39 (3), 301–23.

Nelson, R.E. (1989) 'The strength of strong ties: Social networks and intergroup conflict in organizations'. *Academy of Management Journal*, 32 (2), 377–401.

Patton, M.Q. (1990) *Qualitative Evaluation and Research Methods*. 2nd ed. Newbury Park, CA: Sage.

Penuel, W.R., Fishman, B.J., Cheng, B.H., and Sabelli, N. (2011) 'Organizing research and development at the intersection of learning, implementation, and design'. *Educational Researcher*, 40 (7), 331–7.

Putnam, R.D. (1993) *Making Democracy Work: Civic traditions in modern Italy.* Princeton, NJ: Princeton University Press.

— (1995) 'Bowling alone: America's declining social capital'. *Journal of Democracy*, 6 (1), 65–78.

Rogers, E.M. (1995) *Diffusion of Innovations.* 4th ed. New York: Free Press

Scott, J. (2000) *Social Network Analysis: A handbook.* 2nd ed. London: Sage.

Spradley, J.P. (1980) *Participant Observation.* New York: Holt, Rinehart and Winston.

Stuart, T.E. (1998) 'Network positions and propensities to collaborate: An investigation of strategic alliance formation in a high-technology industry'. *Administrative Science Quarterly*, 43 (3), 668–98.

Tenkasi, R.V., and Chesmore, M.C. (2003) 'Social networks and planned organizational change: The impact of strong network ties on effective change implementation and use'. *Journal of Applied Behavioral Science*, 39 (3), 281–300.

Togneri, W., and Anderson, S.E. (2003) 'How high poverty districts improve'. *Leadership*, 33 (1), 12–16.

Tsai, W. (2000) 'Social capital, strategic relatedness and the formation of intraorganizational linkages'. *Strategic Management Journal*, 21 (9), 925–39.

United States Department of Education (2014) 'Total number of schools in need of improvement'. Online. Accessed via: http://eddataexpress.ed.gov/data-element-explorer.cfm (accessed 12 November 2014).

Yin, R.K. (2003) *Case Study Research: Design and methods.* 3rd ed. Thousand Oaks, CA: Sage

Chapter 12

Reflections on the challenges of leading research and evidence use in schools

Lorna M. Earl

When Chris asked me to consider writing a concluding chapter to identify key themes and gaze into the crystal ball of the future of using evidence in schools, I responded that it sounded like fun. And it has been. The chapters in this edited volume cross so many boundaries – geographical, cultural, political, methodological, and conceptual. Taken together, they illuminate the immense challenges that are associated with something that, on the surface, seems so obvious – using research and evidence for informed decision making in schools. However, as Toby Greany says in Chapter 1, using evidence is actually a messy social process and it plays out at many levels. In this chapter I have tried to make some of the complexity of using evidence for decision making by schools visible and to highlight some of the issues to which schools must attend if they are to be thoughtful and wise consumers and users of evidence.

Context matters

I think it is important to set the discussion of using data or evidence squarely in context. Let me begin with a statement from Chapter 9 by Jonathan Supovitz. He says that:

> 'data use' means different things to decision-makers at different levels of the education system, and that the type and frequency of the data, mode of enquiry, and decision-making processes look quite different according to role, situation, and purpose.
>
> (Chapter 9: 116)

There is an increasing international emphasis on using evidence in decision making to improve teaching practices and raise student achievement. However, how people think about evidence, approach its use, and engage with it are deeply influenced by the context in which it is presented and how they feel about it. In many countries, there are two competing agendas at work. On the one hand, there is a move to hold teachers and schools more externally accountable for the education they provide, using data as evidence of teacher and school effectiveness. This approach is generally associated with top-down (government- or district-driven) external accountability and high-stakes testing. On the other hand, there is a focus on using data as part of evidence-based teacher enquiry, an approach generally associated with bottom-up (teacher-driven), internal (teacher or school) processes and a wide range of sources of evidence (Schildkamp *et al.*, 2013). The chapters in this volume are all written by authors working in the US or the UK, both countries where accountability is high and school leaders and teachers are trying to establish a balance between these, sometimes competing, agendas.

Several chapters in this volume describe examples of evidence use in local contexts using school-based enquiry, in spite of the high-stakes policy environment. The policy context in England is described by Toby Greany: high autonomy is coupled with high accountability for schools, competition among schools is rewarded, and school personnel must second-guess the views of the Inspectorate. However, Taylor and Spence-Thomas (Chapter 10) describe a local initiative that is thriving within this larger national context. Jonathan Supovitz provides another example of a facilitated process in US schools for using data about practice in the form of observations and videotapes as a mechanism for teachers to reflect on what they do and how they do it, even though it is deeply embedded in the No Child Left Behind legislation. These examples are testament to the possibilities for schools to engage in evidence-based enquiry, but other authors in this volume (e.g. Toby Greany in Chapter 1 and Lesley Saunders in Chapter 3) have identified the difficult context within which they are working and point to the long history of attempts to create evidence-based systems that have not always been kind to schools. Lesley Saunders in particular provides a history of evidence use policies in England over several decades that, as she says:

> ... left ... a residue rather than a proper legacy. A major casualty resulting from this is the lack of more nuanced ideas about the relationship between research and teaching ...
>
> (Chapter 3: 42)

As Greany mentions:

> There is growing correlational evidence that where research and evidence are used effectively as part of high-quality initial teacher education and continuing professional development, with a focus on addressing improvement priorities, it makes a positive difference in terms of teacher, school, and system performance.
>
> (Chapter 1: 12)

However, it is not prudent for leaders in schools to ignore the wider context within which they are using evidence. This should not stop them, but rather help them situate their own decision making within the larger landscape of the political and social milieu of schools.

Nature and quality of evidence

It does not make sense to argue about whether or not the use of evidence is valuable. In fact, we have always used evidence. All learning involves engagement with evidence, in the form of knowledge and ideas. The difference in an era of data and research proliferation is that schools have access to a great deal of evidence and research that was not readily available to earlier generations, and much of it comes from outside the local context. Their challenge is one of determining what to pay attention to in the sea of available information from a multitude of known and unknown sources – to establish what counts as evidence in relation to local decision-making needs and to determine how to ascertain quality.

When people think of data, it often conjures up an image of statistics and test scores. Certainly the chapters in this volume from the US provide examples of the pervasiveness of this view. Kara Finnigan and her colleagues (Chapter 11) found that staff in their work had:

> ... a narrow view of evidence, almost exclusively focusing on test scores or other administrative records and outcome data, with few interviewees mentioning practice-oriented or experiential evidence. In fact, several individuals equated 'evidence' and 'research evidence' with standardized test scores.
>
> (Chapter 11: 140)

But there are many other forms of evidence available to schools. Opinions, anecdotes, images, vignettes, and observations are all acceptable as data. Using evidence can involve attending to published research, gathering local data, referring to experts, considering personal experiences, social network analysis, and big data analytics, just to mention a few. However, not all evidence is created equal. One of the first challenges for anyone when they consider evidence as part of their thinking is to ascertain the quality of the evidence that they intend to use. Bad data can contribute to bad decisions.

Tom Bennett (Chapter 2) maintains that no form of evidence is intrinsically bad or good – it merely carries within itself intrinsic strengths and weaknesses. As long as these are borne in mind, by itself no data – if they are honestly harvested – can be dangerous. But Lesley Saunders reminds us:

'Evidence is not all it seems' (Chapter 3: 40). Unfortunately, not all data are honestly harvested.

What does this mean for school leaders? Very simply, 'consumer beware'. Using evidence is a thinking process, where the data or the research provide the tools for thinking. Evidence provides additional information in some area of interest and is only as good as its source, its integrity, and its interpretation. There is a complete science around determining the quality of evidence. In the case of quantitative data, this may involve issues of sampling, or of data collection, or of statistical analysis. With qualitative data, it means considering the perspective and theory behind the work and the care given to alternative interpretations. It is important for school leaders to ask whether the evidence they are considering comes from defensible sources and has integrity, and to have mechanisms for determining the source, credibility, and technical adequacy of the evidence before they use it.

Creating and moving knowledge

Having evidence does not in itself lead to better decision making. Rather, evidence is a catalyst for expanding thinking and moving beyond decisions based on intuition and personal experience. Tom Bennett (Chapter 2) suggests that school leaders and teachers work from a foundation of often unchallenged assumptions, beliefs, and prejudices derived from training and experience that form the tacit knowledge that guides practice. This is consistent with my view, as expressed in a recent chapter:

> Their [teachers] beliefs are usually a composite of intuitive, domain-specific theories that they have constructed on the basis of their everyday experience, and their experience is schools and schooling. These are both created and reinforced by the historical context and by policy expectations, some of which may be competing and inconsistent.
>
> (Earl and Timperley, 2014: 327)

Using evidence for decision making requires intentionally combining tacit and explicit knowledge from evidence and research to come to new insights. For the most part, the chapters in this volume are explicitly set within a frame of learning as a sociocultural process, in which leaders and teachers are actively participating in a cyclical process of considering evidence, sharing ideas, rethinking, and reframing a situation to stimulate and foster innovative solutions to real problems. Like Louise Stoll (Chapter 4), I see this process as one of collective learning that involves generating ideas, challenging assumptions, testing hypotheses, formulating plans, and routinely monitoring progress and making adjustments. This creation of knowledge is not the job of any one individual. It is a social process (Bereiter and Scardamalia, 2003) that requires collective responsibility for accomplishments. As Saunders (Chapter 3) suggests:

> ... the creation of expert professional knowledge is not a matter of 'applying' evidence designed and created elsewhere by others. It is a subtle combination of pre-service training and education, individual and collaborative learning through experience and critical reflection, and immersion in scholarly knowledge.
>
> (Chapter 3: 49)

Viewed through a lens of sociocultural learning theory, leaders and teachers must, as Finnigan and colleagues say, become adept at 'gathering evidence and applying it in a manner that goes beyond superficial use' and move from the role of 'technician and implementer of "research-based evidence," to active generator of knowledge and evidence that can be used to improve school-level outcomes' (Chapter 11: 143). Research and evidence do not answer questions. Meaning comes through the human act of interpretation. Engaging with evidence in this way is an active process (Earl and Katz, 2006) that draws on personal views but also depends upon capturing and organizing ideas in a systematic way, turning the information into meaningful actions, and making the interpretation public and transparent (Senge, 1990).

Leaders create the conditions for faculty to engage in systematic collaborative enquiry using evidence as a professional responsibility, starting from a conviction that there is much to learn, making existing conceptions visible, acquiring new knowledge and skills, and engaging in regular and relentless reflection about what is known, what else we need to know, and how to find out.

Looking forward

In the twenty-first century we are surrounded by data, research, and evidence in every form and at every turn. From analyses of live Twitter feeds to complex problems of microphysics, people everywhere are using data to help them understand their world better. The information explosion is revolutionizing society, with data and information at its heart, and serious issues associated with quality control.

Education is no exception. Educational leaders are inundated with 'evidence' from researchers, policymakers, bloggers, and spin doctors.

This pervasive proliferation of data means that educational decisions will be influenced by data from somewhere. It is not possible to imagine an educational world that does not include appeals to evidence. However, it is possible to envisage an educational system that is ill-equipped to access and engage with valuable evidence in ways that turn it into knowledge, and to use it wisely in the service of good decisions for schools and students. Education is rife with examples of unsophisticated data sets, limited capacity, narrow conceptions of what qualifies as data, and a lack of capacity to use it well (Earl and Louis, 2013). I worry that the educational community is not prepared for the onslaught of data, some of it with questionable integrity and most of it being analysed and interpreted by someone outside education.

Even though I worry, I continue to be cautiously optimistic about school leaders and teachers creating and using knowledge that is grounded in evidence. The chapters in this volume provide many insights into obvious successes and known challenges. But what of the future? The era of unprecedented availability of, and demands for, evidence is already here. It is critical for educators rapidly to become more sophisticated in order to incorporate accurate and defensible evidence into their thinking and to use it appropriately. I see this challenge as one that requires a new mindset, one in which school leaders and teachers are knowledge leaders who enjoy exploring the unknown and thinking in different kinds of ways; appreciate their own knowledge, but also realize how little they know in comparison to all there is to know; constantly question their own assumptions; and avoid strong emotional attachments to any set of beliefs (Bain and Marshall, 2002). With such a mindset, searching out and using high-quality evidence is a necessary part of building new knowledge – considering it, digesting it, debating it, and making meaning from it – within the context of the decisions that school leaders and teachers are trying to make about their practices and their processes.

References

Bain, K., and Marshall, M. (2002) 'Routine vs adaptive expertise'. Online. www.bestteacherinstitute.org/id80.html (accessed 24 November 2014).

Bereiter, C., and Scardamalia, M. (2003) 'Learning to work creatively with knowledge'. In De Corte, E., Verschaffel, L., Entwistle, N., and van Merriënboer, J. (eds) *Powerful Learning Environments: Unraveling basic components and dimensions* (Advances in Learning and Instruction Series). Oxford: Elsevier Science, 55–68.

Earl, L., and Katz, S. (2006) *Leading Schools in a Data-Rich World: Harnessing data for school improvement*. Thousand Oaks, CA: Corwin.

Earl, L., and Louis, K.S. (2013) 'Data use: Where to from here'. In Schildkamp, K., Lai, M., and Earl, L. (eds) *Data-Based Decision Making*. Dordrecht: Springer, 193–204.

Earl, L., and Timperley, H. (2014) 'Challenging conceptions of assessment'. In Wyatt-Smith, C., Klenowski, V., and Colbert, P. (eds) *Designing Assessment for Quality Learning*. Dordrecht: Springer, 325–36.

Schildkamp, K., Lai, M., and Earl, L. (2013) *Data-Based Decision Making*. Dordrecht: Springer.

Senge, P.M. (1990) *The Fifth Discipline: The art and practice of the learning organization*. London: Century Business.

Conclusion

Chris Brown

Engaging with research and evidence as part of a process of effective professional development has substantial benefits for both teacher practice and pupil outcomes. The purpose of this book has been to provide school leaders with a better understanding of how to harness these benefits. As I outline in the Introduction, true research engagement within and between schools will require school leaders to address both the 'transformational' and 'learning-centred' aspects of becoming research and evidence engaged. With this chapter I draw together the core themes emerging from the book into these two aspects and provide a definitive summary 'checklist' for school leaders seeking to develop their schools as evidence-informed. I begin with two factors that cover the 'transformational' acts of enabling research use to be embedded as an organizational goal. The remaining three checklist items focus on the 'learner-centred' aspects of research engagement: ensuring research and evidence use can lead to improved teaching.

Checklist item ①: Does your approach to research and evidence use demonstrate your own commitment as well as facilitate the efforts of others?

As Clare Roberts outlines in Chapter 8, school leadership must actively and demonstrably buy-in to research and evidence use for it to become part of a school's 'way of life'. This means that school leaders must not only promote the vision for, and develop the culture of, a research-engaged school (including the promotion of the values required for learning communities to operate), they must also provide the necessary resources and supporting structures so that sustained and meaningful research use can become a reality, and resulting changes in practice can be employed widely. For example, they need to make time and space available for teachers to come together, ensure that there is access to research, and, as Tom Bennett highlights in Chapter 2, upskill teachers so that they are able to engage critically with research. Distribution of research leadership can be effective, but teacher-researchers' chances of success must be maximized: the vision for success must be clear and the path for reaching the vision cleared.

It is also important that research use is not simply viewed by school leaders as 'someone else's job'. The active involvement of senior leaders with research activity is vital, because having first-hand involvement and experience in research use ensures that it remains 'top of mind' and so a priority; also that any issues in engaging with research and evidence are encountered first-hand. In addition, involvement enables senior leaders to 'walk the talk', not only to demonstrate their commitment, but also to engage in more learning-centred leadership practices such as 'modelling', 'monitoring', and 'mentoring and coaching' (dialogue), thus ensuring wider buy-in across the school (e.g. Southworth, 2009; Earley, 2013). As Louise Stoll notes in Chapter 5 and Lorna Earl notes in Chapter 12, a key characteristic for senior leaders to model is having an 'enquiry habit of mind': senior leaders actively looking for a range of perspectives, purposefully seeking relevant information from numerous and diverse sources, and continually exploring new ways to tackle perennial problems. Modelling could also materialize in senior leaders registering for their own higher level degrees.

Checklist item ②: Does your approach to research and evidence use have buy-in throughout the school?

A key aspect of many definitions of leadership is that there must be a process of influence. As we see in Kara Finnigan, Alan Daly, and colleagues' chapter (Chapter 11), however, leadership activity as a form of influence can be undertaken by more than just those who possess 'formal' responsibility. This notion is also reflected by Jim Spillane and colleagues (2010), who argue that, perhaps more than formal leaders, it is informal leaders who determine the fate of reform initiatives. As a consequence the implementation of new initiatives, such as research and evidence use, must attend to the informal aspects of an organization: in other words, the organization as lived by organizational members in their day-to-day work life. 'Attending to the informal organization', it is argued, 'we expand our focus beyond formally designated leaders in a school's advice network to also include those individuals who are key advice givers, but who have no formal leadership designation' (Spillane *et al.*, 2010: 30). As Louise Stoll and I argue in Chapter 5, one of the core issues in bridging the gap between evidence and practice is the need to influence teachers' values and beliefs, and change their behaviours. Bringing the informal organization into play means that the vision of a school leader needs to be grounded in collaborative ideals and be consensual. It also means that any vision for research engagement needs 'on the ground' champions, including middle leaders, if it is to be embedded at a deep rather than at a surface level.

Checklist item ③: Does your approach to research and evidence use 'start with the end in mind' and ensure that progress towards this end is tracked?

In both Louise Stoll's chapter (Chapter 4) and that of Carol Taylor and Karen Spence-Thomas (Chapter 8), we are reminded of the need to 'start with the end in mind'. In other words, we need to be clear about intended outcomes before we begin any professional learning activity. There are two key benefits to this approach: first, it provides a point of focus – a goal or vision for which we can strive; second, it provides a way to measure impact and so assess how effective our efforts have been in achieving this vision. I look at each of these in more detail below:

- **Providing a point of focus:** a technique often used within the London Centre for Leadership in Learning is to ask teachers 'what difference do you want to make?' and 'what will success look like?' Specifically, in relation to a given issue of teaching and learning, we encourage teachers to think deeply about what pupils will be 'achieving' and 'doing', 'how pupils will be feeling', 'what pupils will be saying', and 'how pupils will be responding [to potential new initiatives]'. We then ask teachers to repeat the exercise in terms of the actions and behaviours in which they will engage that will lead to this change in pupils. Getting teachers to think about future success in this way means that they come to a common understanding of, and a vision for, what needs to be achieved. This helps to ensure that the views of school leaders and staff are in alignment and provides the foundation for action.
- **Evaluating your efforts:** the next step is to ascertain the current actions and behaviours of pupils and teachers. Crucially, this involves turning each of the changes envisioned above into measurable qualities and gathering 'baseline data' in relation to these, either by harvesting readily available data or by collecting new data. Once vision and baseline have been established, teachers can then engage in learning conversations and practical action (see Checklist item ④). Learning conversations and practical action should be focused: (1) on developing theories of action (TOA) that demonstrate proposed relationships between teacher learning and improved student outcomes, via changes in teaching practice; and (2) on conceiving, trialling, and refining activities to achieve the required changes in practice that will result in improved pupil outcomes. Clearly, practical activity must go hand-in-hand with evaluating how quickly and to what extent this action

is helping teachers move from baseline to vision. And if part of the vision is a more general aspiration for the school to become research-engaged, a proposed scale for measuring this is set out in the chapter I wrote with Sue Rogers (Chapter 6). It is also important to share success with peers and other schools – this is covered in more detail in Checklist item ④.

Following evaluation and sharing, practices should be collaboratively refined, radically changed, or removed as appropriate. This means that research engagement activity should not be considered one-off in nature and must be undertaken within the context of a wider iterative cycle of enquiry and improvement: for example, the Connect to Learn (C2L) approach used by Carol Taylor and Karen Spence-Thomas (Chapter 10).

Checklist item ④: Does your approach to research and evidence use have teacher learning and practice at its core?

As Lesley Saunders argues in Chapter 3, effective research use does not mean replacing teacher knowledge with academic knowledge or with the 'what works' knowledge produced by bodies such as the Education Endowment Foundation. Effective research use actually stems from developing expertise; ensuring that teachers are able to bring together 'what is known' (i.e. formal knowledge) with what they know about their context, their pupils, and what they currently see as effective practice (i.e. their experience and the experience of others). In a similar vein, as we see in Jonathan Supovitz's chapter (Chapter 9), effective data use is that which helps teachers make connections and examine the relationships between what they do (teaching activity) and its outcomes (how students fare in response). Engaging in this type of process, described by Louise Stoll as knowledge 'animation' (Chapter 4) and by Sue Rogers and myself as knowledge 'creation' (Chapter 6), means that teachers have a wider understanding of both the causes of problems relating to teaching and learning *and* TOAs and practical understanding of how these might be addressed.

There is increasing evidence that, when done well, it is professional learning in collaborative communities that is the type of CPD most likely to lead to improvements in both teachers' practice and students' outcomes (Stoll *et al.*, 2006; Vescio *et al.*, 2008; Lomos *et al.*, 2011; Harris and Jones, 2012; Sebba *et al.*, 2012). What makes an effective Professional Learning Community (PLC) is discussed in Chapters 5 to 7, along with examples of PLCs. At the London Centre for Leadership in Learning we have coined the phrase *Research Learning Communities* (RLC) to refer to PLCs that have the specific purpose of increasing research use in schools.[1] A key benefit of the RLC approach can be attributed to the nature of the learning that can take place within them. To maximize the benefits of this learning (i.e. to ensure RLC activity results in the type of knowledge-creation outcomes I mention above), RLC participants need to take part in 'learning conversations': considered, thoughtful (rather than superficial) discussion and challenge, focused on matters of teaching practice, that consider evidence of actual and potential forms of practice and that are undertaken with a view to developing both improved practice (i.e. new approaches to issues) and, as a result, improved outcomes for students. The key characteristics of effective learning conversations can be found in *resource box c.1.*

Following learning conversations, there must be a period of practical activity to allow teachers to trial, refine, and build an understanding of when and how it is appropriate to apply proposed new approaches to issues of teaching and learning (i.e. to develop their expertise). In Hélène Galdin-O'Shea's chapter (Chapter 8), for example, both 'lesson study' and 'joint practice development' are held up as examples of how research-informed ideas can be transformed into research-informed realities. Time to practice means that RLC participants have the opportunity to build school capacity by engaging and sharing their expertise with others (e.g. via processes such as 'modelling', 'monitoring', and 'mentoring and coaching'), who can then also begin to practice what they have learned. This has the added benefit that RLC participants gain further understanding through extended practice.

RESOURCE BOX C.1:
Louise Stoll suggests that the following are features characteristic of high-quality learning conversations between adults:

- **Focus on evidence and/or ideas.** Learning conversations are focused, with the specific focus reflecting one of two important perspectives. First, the conversation's focus can centre on existing and effective practice within the school/network. Second, the conversation reflects ideas about innovation and transformation where, for example, the conversation explores creative ways to engage learners and extend learning. Because the second focus will require elements of the first, many conversations weave these two perspectives together. Both require all those participating in the conversation to be committed to the focus (which in itself will need to be linked to the overall values and vision of the RLC). As we see in Jonathan Supovitz's chapter (Chapter 9), to facilitate this aspect of the learning conversation work may be needed to present evidence in a way that is most useful for teachers.

- **Experience and external knowledge/theory.** Access to outside expertise deepens learning conversations. Whether delivered personally, through writing, or via other media, independent ideas are injected to stimulate reflection, challenge the status quo, and extend thinking. Such ideas can help promote greater depth in conversations. For Research Learning Communities 'formal' knowledge (e.g. academic research) is key and is seen as to have equal importance to practitioner-held knowledge in developing new solutions to issues of teaching and learning. Clearly 'formal' knowledge has to be of high quality, an issue addressed by Tom Bennett in Chapter 2.
- **Protocols and tools.** Learning conversations can often be framed more clearly when supported by frameworks and guidelines that help participants to structure their dialogue and interrogate evidence or ideas. Teachers also need opportunities to look at and discuss 'artefacts' of their practice, not just test results (see Chapter 9).
- **Facilitation.** Facilitation is not the same as external expertise. It can come from inside or outside the group, but it is needed to elicit and support intellectual exchange, as well as to maintain open dialogue and, sometimes, to inject new energy into the conversation. Skilful facilitation can often lead to a productive balance of comfort and challenge.

(Stoll, 2012: 6–12)

Checklist item ⑤: Does your approach to research and evidence ensure that the right people are in the room?

In the same way that the vision of school leaders needs 'on the ground' champions if it is to become embedded at a deeper level, aspects of learner-centric leadership also need support from teachers who agree that specific approaches to improving teaching and learning are required, and are happy to promote them to peers. In Chapter 5, Louise Stoll and I detail how we selected middle leaders for this role, but not just any middle leaders – we wanted those who were keen to tackle and promote evidence-informed change. As we soon discovered, the most effective 'catalysts' were influential within and beyond their schools. This meant that their peers were willing to learn from and engage with them.

The social network analysis (SNA) methods introduced in Chapter 11 (by Kara Finnigan, Alan Daly, and colleagues) provide another way of identifying who has influence in the school. For example, as part of the Research Learning Communities project Toby Greany mentions in Chapter 1, I have used SNA to identify, within the primary schools I am working with, which teachers are most often turned to for support in terms of pedagogic expertise, research-informed advice on teaching and learning, and collaborative activities (such as joint lesson planning, the exchange of teaching materials, etc.). These central and influential people, along with senior leaders in their schools, were then chosen as the project's *evidence champions*. Between 2014 and 2016 we will be regularly bringing together evidence champions within learning communities, carrying out activities designed to help them increase the awareness and use of evidence throughout their schools, and measuring the impact of doing this.

Another way of thinking about 'who is in the room' is to consider what expertise and resources are required to make research engagement happen, and, if necessary, to seek these from external sources. Louise Stoll and I partnered with Challenge Partners in our project, giving the schools involved access to 'formal' research, skilled facilitators, a network of middle leaders that could form an instant learning community covering many sites, and a central coordinating function that could negotiate release and cover across 15 schools, pay cover costs, and help ensure schools were all broadly moving in the same direction at the same time. Louise Stoll also makes the point in Chapter 5 that teachers and leaders need critical friends who will ask challenging questions. As Toby Greany highlights in Chapter 1, academics can ask these questions, and school–university partnerships more generally are now vital in England's increasingly autonomous school system if schools, networks, and clusters are to 'self-improve'. Again, the success of these partnerships will be a function of school leaders who can foster the support required, but who can also ensure adequate time and space is created for researchers and practitioners to come together.

Endnotes
[1] See http://educationendowmentfoundation.org.uk/projects/research-learning-communities/.

References

Earley, P. (2013) *Exploring the School Leadership Landscape: Changing demands, changing realities*. London: Bloomsbury.

Harris, A., and Jones, M. (2012) 'Connect to learn: Learn to connect'. *Professional Development Today*, 14 (4), 13–19.

Lomos, C., Hofman, R.H., and Bosker, R.J. (2011) 'Professional communities and student achievement: A meta-analysis'. *School Effectiveness and School Improvement*, 22 (2), 121–48.

Sebba, J., Kent, P., and Tregenza, J. (2012) *Joint Practice Development (JPD): What does the evidence suggest are effective approaches?* Nottingham: National College for School Leadership and University of Sussex.

Southworth, G. (2009) 'Learning-centred leadership'. In Davies, B. (ed.) *The Essentials of School Leadership*. 2nd ed. London: Sage, 91–111.

Spillane, J., Healey, K., and Kim, C. (2010) 'Leading and managing instruction: Formal and informal aspects of elementary school organization'. In Daly, A. (ed.) *Social Network Theory and Educational Change*. Cambridge, MA: Harvard Education Press, 129–58.

Stoll, L. (2012) 'Stimulating learning conversations'. *Professional Development Today*, 14 (4), 6–12.

Stoll, L., Bolam, R., McMahon, A., Wallace, M., and Thomas, S. (2006) 'Professional learning communities: A review of the literature'. *Journal of Educational Change*, 7 (4), 221–58.

Vescio, V., Ross, D., and Adams, A. (2008) 'A review of research on the impact of professional learning communities on teaching practice and student learning'. *Teaching and Teacher Education*, 24 (1), 80–91.

Index

Index

Index